Resource Management in Developing Countries

Resource Management in Developing Countries

AFRICA'S ECOLOGICAL AND ECONOMIC PROBLEMS

Valentine U. James

BERGIN & GARVEY   New York · Westport, Connecticut · London

Copyright Acknowledgments

The author and publisher are grateful to the following for allowing the use of excerpts from:

Ayadike, Obinna. 1988. "Toxic Terrorism." *West Africa* (June 20): 1108.

Buringh, P. 1979. *Introduction to the Study of Soils in the Tropical and Sub-tropical Regions*. Wageningen, The Netherlands: Center for Agricultural and Publishing Documentation, p. 3.

Food and Agriculture Organization of the United Nations. 1973. *Map of Major Soils of the World*. Paris: FAO, pp. 27-40.

Food and Agriculture Organization of the United Nations, Unesco. 1982. "Population Data of Some African Countries." *FAO Production Yearbook*. Vol. 36. FAO: Rome, p. 62.

Husbands, Winston. 1989. *Annals of Tourism Research* 16 (689). Oxford: England Pergamon Press PLC: p. 240.

The World Bank. 1972. *Tourism: Sector Working Paper*. Washington, D.C.: The World Bank, pp. 30-32.

Library of Congress Cataloging-in-Publication Data

James, Valentine Udoh, 1952–
    Resource management in developing countries : Africa's ecological and economic problems / Valentine U. James.
        p.   cm.
    Includes bibliographical references and index.
    ISBN 0-89789-224-0 (alk. paper). — ISBN 0-89789-227-5 (pbk. : alk. paper)
    1. Natural resources—Africa—Management.   I. Title.
    HC800.Z65J35   1991
    333.7′096—dc20   90-49217

British Library Cataloguing in Publication Data is available.

Library of Congress Catalog Card Number: 90-49217
ISBN: 0-89789-224-0 (hb.)
        0-89789-227-5 (pbk.)

First published in 1991

Bergin & Garvey, One Madison Avenue, New York, NY 10010
An imprint of Greenwood Publishing Group, Inc.

Printed in the United States of America

The paper used in this book complies with the
Permanent Paper Standard issued by the National
Information Standards Organization (Z39.48-1984).

10   9   8   7   6   5   4   3   2   1

To

MELANIE,

MY WIFE,

AND MARSHALL AND JONATHAN,

MY SONS

CONTENTS

TABLES AND FIGURES

TABLES

FIGURES

ABBREVIATIONS

CGIAR	Consultative Group on International Agricultural Research
FAO	Food and Agriculture Organization
GDP	Gross domestic product
GNP	Gross national product
ICRISAT	International Crop Research Institute for the Semi-Arid Tropics
IITA	International Institute of Tropical Agriculture
ILCA	International Livestock Center for Africa
ILRAD	International Laboratory for Research on Animal Diseases
IMF	International Monetary Fund
INRA	Institute for Natural Resources in Africa
ITTA	International Tropical Timber Agreement
ITTO	International Tropical Timber Organization
NIEO	New International Economic Order
OAU	Organization for African Unity
UN	United Nations
UNDP	United Nations Development Program
UNEP	United Nations Environmental Program
URADP	Upper Regional Agricultural Development Program
WARDA	West Africa Rice Development Association
WFP	World Food Program
WHO	World Health Organization

PREFACE

The major thrust of this book is pragmatic, interdisciplinary, and academic, and is intended to reach a wide range of audiences, such as educators, students, planners, middle-range policymakers of developing countries, and private and public international organizations that have been puzzled with Africa's declining resource base.

This book makes no assumptions about the reader's knowledge of Africa's geography, history, or political, social, ecological, and economic situations. Rather, it attempts to explain and shed light on areas pertinent to the question of resource management.

The subject of resource management in the developing countries is now receiving more attention than ever before, mainly because of the recurrent catastrophes that have plagued the developing countries in the last two decades. These problems cover a wide range of disciplines, such as the natural sciences, politics, economics, and sociocultural aspects. In order to fully comprehend these problems, one needs to begin to seek answers by investigating the causes of the problems. The linkages between the different facets of resource management must be fully examined before solutions can be sought.

Eight of the eleven chapters of this book specifically address the concerns of the four disciplines mentioned earlier. Their central ideas, while specific, are complementary. It is the aim of this book to shed some light on the problem by explaining the reasons why and how the problem of resource management manifests itself. Pertinent case studies are cited where appropriate in order to substantiate the arguments made about the decline in biological diversity and about human potential, political instability, economic woes, and sociocultural decay. Possible solutions are suggested and inferences are drawn. It is the hope of the author that the book will be useful to policymakers, planners, economists, political leaders, academics, and students of Third World development planning.

ACKNOWLEDGMENTS

This book began as a result of the University of California President's Postdoctoral Fellowship Award. The award gave me the time and resources necessary to conduct research and write about issues of resource management in developing countries. Hence acknowledgment must go to those officials of the University of California system who recognize the importance of diversifying academic settings in order to embrace all of our society.

Particular thanks to my mentor, Dr. Christine Schonewald-Cox, who provided answers to many questions about resource management. She made the fellowship experience worthwhile and prepared me for academic life in a research institution.

I have had the opportunity to discuss the issues raised in this book with many scholars at conferences and at the University of Southwestern Louisiana, where I taught for three years. I thank them all for giving of their valuable time to broaden my perspective on the issues of resource development in the emerging nations of the world.

My wife and children have been very understanding and cooperative during the whole process of writing this book. I thank them for sharing the excitement, worries, fears, and chores of the academic profession.

Many thanks to Peggy Vincent for the tremendous work of typing the final draft of the manuscript and for assisting with the cumbersome work of indexing.

Finally, acknowledgment is due my editor, Sophy Craze, for being patient with me and for her encouragement and editorial comments during the process of writing this book.

1 INTRODUCTION: THE LEGACY OF COLONIALISM

In the 1980s, the plight of suffering Africans received more attention than ever before. There were many sympathetic responses to starving and dying Africans. Food aid and loans were given, and in some countries aid is still being distributed to alleviate the problem of hunger. But the root of hunger lies in the fact that it is human made—by both the international and the African communities. The African ecosystem has been violated through overexploitation, and, as a result, the flora and fauna that constitute some of the greatest ecological diversity in the world have declined.

The discussions presented in this book explore the current condition of the resource management problem in Africa, detail the present trend and the possible end result, and suggest some solutions. The deteriorating environmental conditions due to overexploitation of natural resources culminates in low fertility of African soils, erosion, deforestation, and desertification.

The topic of resource management in developing countries is complex, covering many subjects or disciplines. Resource management demands a thorough understanding of the different facets of a given society in which the natural resource is available. Thus, an attempt has been made in this book to give a multidisciplinary overview that is not simplistic in its description, analysis, and synthesis of the growing problem. This book is written to address the concerns of decision makers, planners, international organizations, and private individuals. It is meant to give an African perspective of the dwindling resource base in Africa.

The image that many Europeans and other Westerners have of Africa is that it is a continent of jungles where wild animals roam freely and where the inhabitants are impoverished. On the contrary, in terms of its natural resources, Africa happens to be one of the wealthiest continents. The tropical rain forest of Africa contains diverse flora and fauna communities that can only be rivaled by those of the South American and Asian tropics. It is too often forgotten that many of the raw materials that are used in the industrialized countries come from Africa and the rest of the developing world. The question then is why the poorest peoples are found in one of the wealthiest continents.

One can rightfully argue that Africa's problems began after the 1885 Congress of Berlin divided the African continent into partitions that suited the colonial powers (Figure 1). The countries that obtained their independence during the 1960s and 1970s (Figure 2) emerged out of the past partition. Generally, these countries had no past (traditional) concept of national wealth and power. Unfortunately, history shows that Africans had many great empires, such as the Ghana and the Moorish empires. The great civilizations of the Egyptians and the Ethiopians have given the world the foundations of leadership in government. The interests of Africa were not pursued by the colonial masters, and many of the natural resources were exploited by them. For example, wildlife such as elephants were hunted down for their tusks, and lions were seriously reduced in numbers for their hides. The past indiscriminate logging of African timber and mining of natural resources for industries in the Western world were the beginning of the decline of ecological diversity in Africa.

Another argument concerning the decline of the natural resources in Africa is that during the years following independence, many African nations mismanaged their natural resources and abused the environment, and the exponential increase in population has put pressures on marginal lands. Thus, it appears that Africa's problems have originated from the mistakes of the European mapmakers (Conference of 1885), from subsequent exploitation, and from the fact that the emerging nations put great effort into becoming nations while carelessly exploiting natural resources.

The consequences of lack of planning and of strategies to manage and use Africa's resources have resulted in deforestation, desertification, food shortages, soil erosion, and decline in biological diversity. Some African nations with policies and programs to deal with resource management have difficulties implementing them. The severe transformation of the savanna ecosystems has exacerbated the drought problems that Africa has faced in the 1970s and 1980s and will probably still face in the 1990s. This has resulted in the hunger situation in Africa. By 1984, it was estimated that about twenty-six African countries were seriously affected by acute food shortages, although, because the continent is endowed with vast natural resources, African countries should be able to feed their people and have substantial amounts of food crops left over to export to other countries.

Figure 1
The Division of Africa (1885)

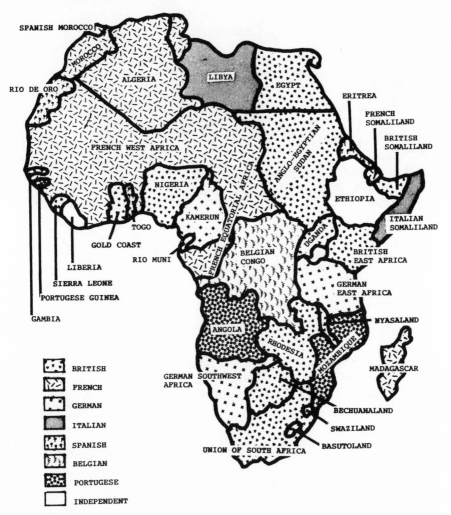

SPANISH MOROCCO

MOROCCO

RIO DE ORO

ALGERIA

LIBYA

EGYPT

ERITREA

FRENCH SOMALILAND

BRITISH SOMALILAND

FRENCH WEST AFRICA

ANGLO-EGYPTIAN SUDAN

NIGERIA

KAMERUN

ETHIOPIA

ITALIAN SOMALILAND

TOGO

FRENCH EQUATORIAL AFRICA

UGANDA

GOLD COAST

RIO MUNI

BELGIAN CONGO

BRITISH EAST AFRICA

LIBERIA

SIERRA LEONE

PORTUGESE GUINEA

GERMAN EAST AFRICA

GAMBIA

NYASALAND

ANGOLA

RHODESIA

MOZAMBIQUE

MADAGASCAR

BRITISH

FRENCH

GERMAN

ITALIAN

SPANISH

BELGIAN

PORTUGESE

INDEPENDENT

GERMAN SOUTHWEST AFRICA

BECHUANALAND

SWAZILAND

BASUTOLAND

UNION OF SOUTH AFRICA

In order for African countries to be stable economically and politically, they must find the ways and means of securely controlling the use of their natural resources. In other words, African nations must establish the necessary network and skills and thoroughly coordinate them to exploit the resources in perpetuity. There must be an awareness that the resources should not be wasted or abused. With careful analyses of present problems and implementation of policies to correct problems, African societies can be successful in the modern world. These policies do not have to be limited to domestic problems; they should include international problems, es-

Figure 2
The Independent Countries of Africa (1960 and after)

pecially those that have to do with the developed countries. For instance, African countries are treated unfairly by the prices the industrialized nations offer for African natural resources, and many African countries find it difficult to export their products because of custom barriers imposed by the developed countries.

In an attempt to address African problems, international organizations, banks, and individual Western countries have been providing aid meant to improve the situation. A warning came after the Food and Agriculture Organization's (FAO) regional conference for Africa in 1986: The conclusion was reached that if present deteriorating agricultural situations, environmental degradation, and economic crisis continue in Africa, the continent's future will be jeopardized by widespread chronic famine.

There is much debate over the role of foreign aid in the development of Africa. Some researchers contend that one cannot make a judgment about whether or not foreign aid has improved Africa's deteriorating agricultural and economic development. Others contend that without the aid, the problems could be worse. There is another group of scholars who argue that foreign aid only gives temporary solutions without considering the long-term effect, and that foreign aid has actually exacerbated the problem. The summation of the views expressed in this book is that aid is needed and that the aid should be directed toward appropriate projects that consider African interests. It is certainly true that when aid is poorly planned and organized, problems become worse. Then aid only gives temporary success, while in the long run the problems it brings have been documented to be overwhelming in certain areas of Africa. For example, it is well known that previous efforts to stop the famine crisis in the Sahelian region failed because they were aimed at stopping short-term problems. Aid monies or loans are usually for designated export products, thereby neglecting the production of food crops. The situation in the Sahel has not improved despite increased outside assistance.

The bad financial situation of many African countries has made the operation and maintenance of projects related to natural resources difficult. Many of these countries are in great debt to the industrialized countries. The debts of African nations represent substantial portions of the gross national products (GNP) of these countries. Since some of these debts are owed to multilateral institutions, such as the World Bank, whose loans are designated to specific projects, African nations are not able to pursue their own interests. Besides, the interest rates on these loans are very high. Some of these countries cannot pay the interest on the loans. For example, 60 percent of Ghana's foreign earnings in 1986 are equivalent to the payment on the debt service, while the remaining 40 percent is equivalent to the amount that can be used for the importation of oil. The current pattern of food aid causes serious distortions in African economies. It is also important to recognize that food aid is a damaging disincentive to the production of food in developing countries. It leads to dependence on food aid and commercial food imports.

The attempts toward sustainable development in Sub-Saharan Africa will depend on intelligent, unified efforts on a regional basis. African farmers are facing a time in history when adjustments need to be made in order to produce enough food for Africans. African governments will have to devise food policies that can encourage farmers. Nigerian agriculture faced a 0.6 percent decline in growth rate between 1971 and 1981, while its annual population increase is 2.5 percent. Food policies, if correctly implemented to include investment in land and water development, can reverse the current situation. There have been predictions by the FAO (*West Africa* 1986) about the deplorable situation in Africa. One such prediction is that because of so much desertification in Nigeria, it will be almost impossible for it to be self-sufficient again. Nonetheless, African countries appear to be committing themselves to new goals and objectives; with good leadership, they can save the continent from what appears, from overseas, to be a disastrous course. Some agricultural successes are scattered all over Africa. But efforts should be made to ensure their continuation and emulation.

The FAO spends about 40 percent of its budgets on activities in Africa, and in 1986 it raised close to $215 million from bilateral and multilateral donors. If the money spent in Africa is set up so that rural farmers' needs are met through projects that upgrade rural infrastructure and build up the necessary support systems (not bureaucracies), then progress in Africa will begin.

Educators and scholars of Third World development have always expressed concern about the lack of understanding of the negative impact of colonialism on African countries. Students and colleagues who have had little training in this area often wonder why, after all this time following independence, African countries have not made significant strides in their development efforts.

In order to create understanding, one needs to explain the many facets of colonialism and its linkages to development or underdevelopment. Ashcraft (1973:7) explains the difference between underdevelopment and underdeveloped countries by contending that the existence of relative poverty conditions in countries of the Third World qualify them as underdeveloped countries, while the political and economic ramifications that enhance the emergence or emanation of such conditions is referred to as underdevelopment.

Since independence many African countries have had several coups and changes of government with policies, goals, objectives, and strategies aimed at progress of development. They have faced many difficulties and, in many instances, their development programs have failed. One should understand that since these programs are linked to the assistance and help of developed nations who have a distinct competitive edge economically and technologically, African countries will continue to have problems. There is a correlation between the African problems of today and colonialism. The disadvantaged position of African countries has resulted in their continued lack of market opportunities.

Historically, colonial governments (British, French, German, Portuguese, Italian, and Belgian) were more interested in controlling the resources of the African countries than in making African countries strong self-sufficient entities. In order to achieve this goal, they paid more attention to the stability of the labor markets in African countries and to the enforcement of colonial law and order. Enclaves that suited the needs of the colonial settlers were formed, and very little was done for the developmental purposes of the African countries.

In the competitive world of today, one notices the same process going on because the developed nations still do things that favor them when dealing with the disadvantaged African nations. But before examining the issues of assistance (aid) and flow of private foreign capital to African countries, the historical perspective of colonialism should be examined.

Colonialists have argued that they brought a great deal of progress—development—to Africa. However, opponents contend that the intensification of colonial activities—exploitation—is not progress. Certainly, Africa had some sort of development going on in the continent before the arrival of Europeans. It is argued by authors such as Rodney (1974:224) that colonization interrupted the natural progress of development that Africa was undergoing, and that progress was stopped in some countries and completely reversed in others.

Although the duration of European colonization of Africa was slightly less than three decades, the negative impact was enormous in the sense that it was during this period that the rest of the world was making significant leaps in development (Rodney 1974). Rodney argues that colonialism caused Africa to lose its power to determine its destiny and to bargain for its natural resources (which Europe needed). The colonial period made it impossible for African people to have control over their economic, political, and social future. Rodney (1974:224) contends:

It [colonialism] meant a tendency towards direct appropriation by Europeans of the social institutions within Africa. Africans ceased to set indigenous cultural goals and standards, and lost full command of training young members of the society. Those were undoubtedly major setbacks.

It is impossible for any group of people who are colonized to be active participants in the history of the world. The political implication is that colonization destroyed the existing political apparatus and replaced it with what suited the European colonialist. The great empires of Songhei and Sudan passed on traditional ruling ideas to authentic African rulers. Colonialism destroyed those ideas; in some cases traditional rulers were kept as mere figureheads to report to the colonial masters. This was an indirect way of controlling the general population (Rodney 1974:225).

Discussion of resource management in Africa must touch upon African technology. Precolonial history indicates that there was some technological development in Africa before the arrival of Europeans. People learned to be blacksmiths, carpenters, architects, and artisans. The arrival of Europeans on the continent brought some difficulties in the indigenous technological aspects of the continent. Rodney (1974:221) notes:

In North Africa, handicraft industries had made the greatest advances before colonialism, in spheres ranging from brasswork to woolens. . . . But French colonialism destroyed the handicraft industries and threw thousands out of work. . . .
In Africa it was simply destruction without redress. By the time political independence was achieved, surviving craftsmanship had been turned towards attracting
tourists rather than meeting the real needs of African people.

The impact of colonialism on African technology was not only the displacement of thousands of workers but the shift of emphasis in African
technology from developing ideas from scratch to working for Europeans
on a basis that benefited European economy.

Technology is part of the culture of a society. Technology that is based
on an authentic culture is easy to pass on to younger generations. Just like
language, such a technology could have been easy to document, learn, and
incorporate into the educational curricula of Africa. The introduction of
European-based technology slowed down the process of development of
authentic African technology. The cost of transfer of European technology is still very expensive, and one can imagine the problems introducing
foreign technology has brought upon African nations—especially that of
dependency, which is discussed in a later chapter.

Whether formal or informal, education existed in Africa before the arrival of Europeans. Informal education was linked to the social and economic fabric of African life. The pattern of learning in informal settings is
part of a natural developmental process; children naturally emulate their
parents and elders. Family gatherings were places where ideas were ex-
changed, children were taught, and leadership roles were learned. The
educational process involved emotional, spiritual, and psychological facets
of African life as well as the intellectual.

Every member of a family and/or extended family knew exactly what
his or her role was in the instillation of values in the younger generation.
These values determined how the resources of the community were allocated, how labor was distributed, and how resources were managed so that
they could be utilized indefinitely.

In conjunction with informal education, formal education existed during the precolonial period. Because the teachers usually were also members of the village, they tended to put a great deal of effort and energy
into the training of the young men and women of the village. A moral
commitment existed; the teachers were well known to the parents of the
pupils.

Colonial education lacked the personal qualities of precolonial education. Rodney (1974:240–41) places colonial education in its true perspective when he notes:

The colonizers did not introduce education into Africa: they introduced a new set of formal educational institutions which partly supplemented and partly replaced those which were there before. . . . The main purpose of colonial school systems was to train Africans to help man the local administration at the lowest ranks and to staff the private capitalist firms owned by Europeans. . . . Colonial education was a series of limitations inside other limitations. The first practical limitation was politico-financial, which means that political policy, rather than the actual availability of money, guided financial expenditure. . . . The closer one scrutinizes the educational contribution of colonialism even in purely quantitative terms the more it shrinks into insignificance.

The European educational system meant that new methods of instruction had to be learned, which slowed down the natural development of the educational system. Because it was not linked to the African social system, this colonial educational system led to the increase of disorder in the African society. Hence, the introduction of a European-style judicial system was meant to bring about order, hence decreasing the emerging disorder (entropy).

For many decades before the arrival of Europeans, Africans managed their domestic affairs with the use of traditional judicial systems based on authentic African laws and regulations. The traditional rulers played significant and prominent roles in maintaining law and order.

Foreign judicial systems were introduced into the African countries that were colonized by Europeans. The introduction of foreign judicial systems brought its own set of problems to Africa. It is important to stress these problems because they outweigh the benefits. Africa had to learn the new judicial systems and abandon (to a degree) their traditional systems of law. This strategy slowed down the progress already made, and the period of transition was marked by many difficulties in administering the correct and appropriate justice to the citizens of many African countries.

In some African countries like Nigeria and Sudan, the British common law system and the traditional African law system are employed. This creates a number of problems, such as corruption, bureaucracy, and complexity in the judicial system. Many African countries have been left with a confused system because the governments of some countries like Nigeria are still struggling with the problem of balancing the traditional judicial system and the English-style judicial system, enabling it to administer justice to the citizens.

An examination of the political problems in Africa shows that very few countries have had stable governments since independence. This is a clear indication of what results when colonialism brings people of diverse linguistic groups together by destroying their traditional ruling systems. Since their independence, Africans are still redefining how to govern themselves in the "modern" world.

In order to appreciate the impact of colonialism on urban and regional development of Africa, it is imperative to understand how different the economic structure of African cities and villages during the precolonial days were from European cities. In general, cities develop along a gradient of economic activities and social phenomena. The pattern of development for African cities did not necessarily involve monetary exchange, unlike colonialism, and hence this change affected urban development. It became necessary to imitate the development patterns of Europe in order to meet the goals and objectives of the colonialists. These goals and objectives were not necessarily in favor of African countries. Countries were divided into regions to harness natural resources for administrative purposes. For example, Nigeria was divided into a northern region, a western region, and an eastern region. Today, Nigeria is still struggling with the question of how many states it should have in order to satisfy its citizens and to rule and develop the country effectively.

During the colonial era, employment opportunities were created in a few urban centers of Africa by the colonial rulers. The office jobs in the urban centers exacerbated the problem of migration from the rural areas to the cities. Since very little planning was done for housing of the new population, squatter settlements began to emerge in and around the urban centers. Squatter settlements constitute one of Africa's most serious problems because they make the planning of infrastructure development very difficult and the provision of services such as water, electricity, and sewage systems is almost impossible. The cities of Freetown, Lagos, Accra, and Lome all have slums that have emerged as a very serious problem.

Colonialism established a trend of exploitation of the natural resources of Africa. This trend began when Europeans discovered that the hides, skins, tusks, and furs of animals found in developing nations could be acquired cheaply and then sold in Europe and America for high prices. This action accelerated the decline of the biological diversity of the African savannas and forests.

In modern-day Africa, poachers kill the most majestic and harmless of beasts with weapons made in foreign countries. These poachers are greedy and, worst of all, are better armed than the wardens of the parks where the elephants and other animals of the wild roam. Poachers have killed several thousands of elephants in order to support the trade of illegal ivory. Recent estimates indicate that there are fewer than 500,000 elephants in Africa (*Science News* 1988). This alarming situation has made governments and conservationists take action to reverse the situation. In Kenya recently, the government publicly burned elephant tusks in order to protest the illegal ivory trade. This action attracted international attention and has resulted in some countries banning the importation of ivory products. Japan is said to be one of the biggest importers of ivory products. International cooperation is needed in order to stop the destruction of the wildlife in Africa. Trading in ivory must be made illegal, and assistance should be given to governments to combat the poachers and to provide well-managed parks for wildlife.

The rhinoceros represents another member of the animal kingdom that is seriously endangered. These animals are represented by five species— white, Sumatran, Indian, Javan, and black. Black rhinoceroses numbered about 65,000 in Africa twenty-five years ago; unfortunately, senseless exploitation of these magnificent animals has reduced the number to about 4,000. The majority of this remaining number is limited to Zimbabwe (*Sports Illustrated* 1987). The rhinoceroses are also exploited for their horns, which contain ingredients used for medicinal purposes in East Asia.

As in the case of the elephants, it is suggested that international cooperation is needed to reverse this situation as quickly as possible, otherwise the black rhinoceros will be extinct by the year 2000.

2 THREATS TO ECOLOGICAL SYSTEMS

Moorman and Greenland (1980) argue that most traditional systems of agriculture in developing countries are closely related to the environment because productivity is not intensified, but when these systems of agricultural practices are intensified and coupled with inadequate management, the ecological systems in the developing countries suffer great destruction. The conversion of ecological systems is further exacerbated by the introduction of large-scale capital-intensive agricultural systems. The conversion of the forests and savannas of Africa began with the introduction of large-scale agricultural systems by Europeans.

Several researchers have clearly indicated that human activities have accelerated the pace of ecological conversion (destruction) as far back as the early 1600s (Forsberg 1977). The awareness has not generated research efforts that would provide enough data about the ecological problems in developing countries.

In Africa, South America, and parts of Asia, the ecological problems can be categorized into three basic interrelated groups:

1. The geometric increase in human population—surpassing the carrying capacity of the finite resources.

2. Inadequate food production resulting from the focus on production of cash crops and the migration of young men, who could be helping with rural agriculture, to urban centers.

3. Deteriorating rural and urban environments.

These problems occur within an ecological framework that has not been adequately tackled by researchers. One of the many areas of prevailing ignorance is the ecological importance of environmental degradation due to subsistence agriculture, commercial agriculture, livestock ranching, forest utilization, and subsistence hunting. Most subsistence agriculture demands the slash-and-burn technique, which entails the cutting down of trees and bush and clearing of land. This results in an immediate enrichment of the soil. But accompanying this process is the exposure of the soil to the torrential rains of the tropics. In some places, such as the Imo State of Nigeria, erosion problems result from human activities. Commercial agriculture and livestock ranging in many parts of the developing world do not take into consideration the "connection principle" of environmental planning and management. The connection principle states that everything is connected to everything else. Livestock ranching, forest utilization, and subsistence hunting should be done in moderation and with the understanding that if carried out in excess, biological diversity could be in danger because less diverse ecological systems are very fragile and cannot withstand human disturbance.

To the knowledge of this researcher, no concerted effort has been made to relate the systems of African farming to the problems resulting from such practices. This chapter is an attempt to fill the gap in the literature with an agro-ecological approach to assessing human impact on the ecological systems in developing countries. There are many reasons why agricultural production in Africa has not kept pace with the population growth. Among these reasons are the agricultural policies of many African countries. Other reasons include past colonial policies and the failure of farming as a profession to attract young Africans. The human disturbance of the ecosystems in the developing nations has created a need for serious land use planning and environmental management methodologies that are not only sound but also economically and socially viable in these countries.

AGRO-ECOLOGICAL MODELS IN AFRICA

History has shown that humans have always used intellectual ability to modify the biological equilibrium for their benefits. Agricultural practices all over the world have enhanced people's ability to find nourishment, and thus humankind has managed to survive in a world of serious competition where only the strongest survive. However, farming practices have also caused environmental problems. It is of interest to examine some of the models that have been advanced to study agro-ecological systems, particularly regarding European and African influences on the ecological systems of Africa. The model in this study is supported with limited data and represents the author's understanding of the circumstances surrounding African agricultural systems and mechanized agriculture. The model is of value in deepening the theoretical understanding of economic, sociological, and environmental factors.

The model suggested by Duncan (1969) emphasizes the argument that environment, population, technology, and organization are the fundamental factors influencing the sociological and spatial diversity of a society. Lambooy (1969) argues that along with all the factors mentioned by Duncan, there is a fifth factor—namely "the pattern of culture of the people under consideration" (Figure 3). The model of an ecological system is presupposed to be in a dynamic equilibrium and a change in any of the five factors causes a shift in the balance of the system. However, the model allows for stress and tension due to endogenous factors, that is, those caused by humans (Raay 1975). The model enhances the researcher's ability to investigate the relationship between any two of the five factors shown in Figure 3. The model is also a unifying mechanism for interdisciplinary contribution.

The agro-ecological model proposed in this chapter could be described as being restrictive because it considers the three main agents of conversion of forests and savannas. The agents are

Figure 3
Schematic Representation of the Components of an Ecological Setting

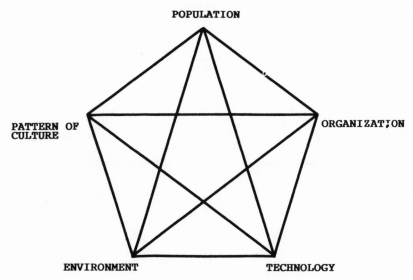

Source: Raay, H.G.T. van. 1975. *Rural Planning in a Savanna Region.* Rotterdam, The Netherlands: Rotterdam University Press, p. 12.

1. the commercial timber harvester,
2. the forest and savanna farmer, and
3. the cattle rancher.

Conversion, as used by the author in this study, means disruption, degradation, impoverishment, and/or destruction of primary forest. Figure 4 is a schematic model extending the model advanced by Lambooy. Human activities based on sociocultural background have some benefits and costs; hence people are confronted with the problem of making appropriate choices. The alternatives available have environmental consequences.

The poverty that confronts many developing nations forces their inhabitants to disregard the importance of the natural order. The adoption of policies that have detrimental effects on the ecosystems of their countries makes the environmental situation worse. Figure 5 is an attempt to schematically depict the cycle of destruction that the ecological systems of developing nations are exposed to because of the decline in economic situation, government policies, and cultural/social values.

Figure 4
Cost-Benefit Analysis and Environmental Degradation

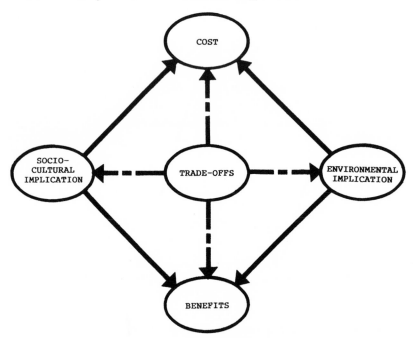

Figure 5
Economic Decline and Environmental Degradation

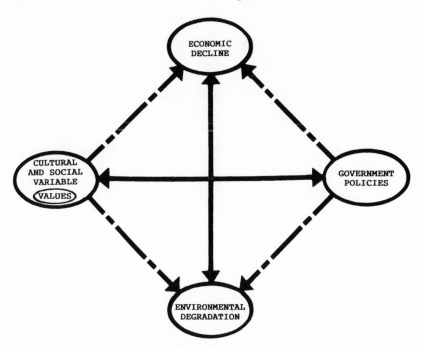

AFRICAN FARMING SYSTEMS

Since environmental ramifications are highlighted in this chapter, it is pertinent to give an overview of the agricultural systems in the developing countries.

The farming systems in Africa are difficult to classify because each has its own set of objectives and goals. The agricultural systems are even more difficult to categorize because of environmental factors associated with each. These factors include soil, water, and microclimate. Other factors that complicate the classification problem are biological and socioeconomic in nature. Hence, farming practices appear to be site specific. Nevertheless, a few attempts have been made, by researchers such as Spedding (1975), Morgan and Pugh (1969), Floyd (1969), and Okigbo (1980), to classify the agricultural systems in Africa. Table 1 is a classification of the traditional agricultural systems in Africa.

Often connected with the traditional agricultural systems is the fact that the biological systems (biomes) have experienced a long history of clearance and disturbance by man; unfortunately, there has been a poor understanding of the ecological and economic consequences of such actions.

Table 1
Classification of Traditional Farming Systems in Africa

---

1.   (a)   Nomadic Herding

       (b)   Shifting Cultivation

2.   Bush Fallowing or Land Rotation (shifting cultivation)

3.   Rudimentary Sedentary Agriculture (shifting cultivation)

4.   Compound Farming and Intensive Subsistence Agriculture

       (shifting cultivation)

5.   Mediterranean Agriculture

Agricultural systems in many developing countries have a long history of tradition and custom. They have survived mainly on the basis of trial and error—often at the expense of the biological systems (Coursey 1976). Shaw (1968, 1972, 1976), Haviden (1975), Harris (1976), and Harlan, DeWet, and Stember (1976) generally agree that the agricultural systems of many developing nations have been greatly influenced by techniques from more advanced nations. Figure 6 is an attempt to show the predominant farming systems in Africa. It should be pointed out that other types of farming systems may be carried out in the different regions along with the predominant ones—nomadic herding, shifting cultivation, and bush fallowing.

Farming systems in Africa are still evolving because of influences from more technologically advanced nations where mechanized agriculture is practiced. Although mechanization of agriculture has enhanced agricultural production in some African countries, it has also produced some problems. In countries like Sierra Leone, it has been known that the mechanization of rice production increased erosion problems. Other factors contributing to the evolution of the agricultural systems in Africa are population increases, the availability of potential markets, and the demand for food generated by the increase in urbanization (Okigbo 1980). A typical farm in Africa can generally be described as small—about five acres or less. Cultivation is performed with primitive tools and much human labor. Cultivation on a permanent basis is carried out on a compound farm; from these centers of activity merge roads and pathways. It is well worth mentioning that cultivation on this type of farm is intensive, a widespread farming method in Africa. An important feature of the compound farm is a series of short-term fallow rotations. Tree crops or a mix-

Figure 6
Agricultural Systems in Africa

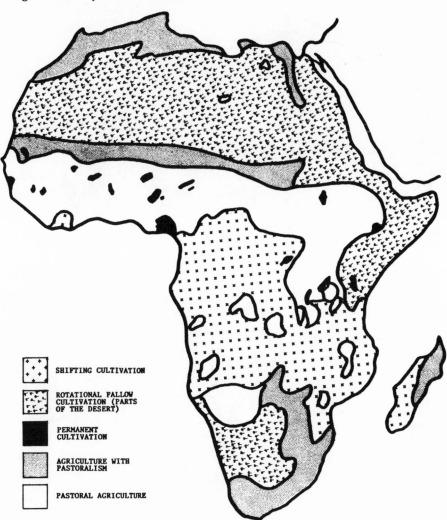

SHIFTING CULTIVATION

ROTATIONAL FALLOW
CULTIVATION (PARTS
OF THE DESERT)

PERMANENT
CULTIVATION

AGRICULTURE WITH
PASTORALISM

PASTORAL AGRICULTURE

ture of crop plants are planted in many of these. In Africa, it is not uncommon to find field systems consisting of bush fallows of varying duration. All traditional systems of agriculture make use of the opportunities offered by nature, including topography, rainfall, and microclimate. The main features of African vegetation, as shown in Figure 7, are forest, grasslands, and deserts. The first two are slowly being converted into the third. What is left in Africa today in terms of forests and savannas is what

Figure 7
Vegetation Zones of Africa

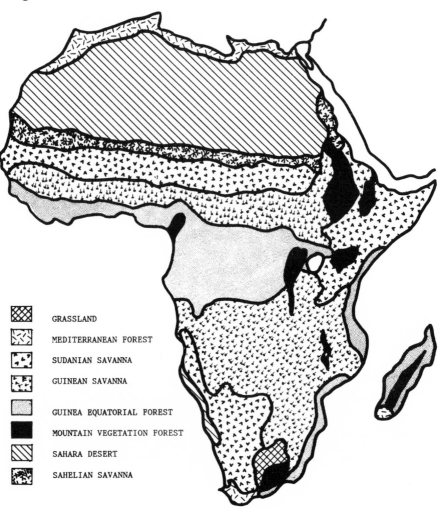

GRASSLAND

MEDITERRANEAN FOREST

SUDANIAN SAVANNA

GUINEAN SAVANNA

GUINEA EQUATORIAL FOREST

MOUNTAIN VEGETATION FOREST

SAHARA DESERT

SAHELIAN SAVANNA

nature has managed to save despite the abuse and mismanagement of these resources (Kimble 1960).

Nomadic agriculture in Africa entails the movement of herds from one place to another—usually north or south according to the rainfall and the availability of vegetation. In the past, when territorial boundaries were not taken seriously by African nations and the population of many African countries was relatively low, nomadic herding did not pose a significant threat to the ecosystem. In modern-day Africa, the problems associated with nomadic agriculture are enormous. The increasing population in many African countries reduces the range for the nomads to travel with their cattle. The cattle, sheep, and other animals need fresh grass year round. With urbanization, the nomadic way of life competes directly with modern lifestyles in Africa. It is not uncommon in Kano, Ibadan, and Kaduna (Nigeria) for one to see a nomadic farmer holding traffic so that his cattle can cross the street. It is also clear that with increasing desertification, nomadic life is in great jeopardy. That means that African countries have to develop policies and programs that will help the nomads obtain a more sedentary lifestyle.

A typical traditional African farm is complex because it can be composed of a compound farm, several field systems of arable food or export crops, and other patchy farms.

Okigbo (1980:147) notes that traditional agricultural systems in Africa generally involve the following:

1. Land development and preparation.
2. Cultivations.
3. Cropping patterns.
4. Miscellaneous cultural practices such as weeding, mulching, and fertilizer application.
5. Pest, weed, and disease control.
6. Harvesting and grazing.
7. Processing and utilization.

Agricultural practice in many developing nations is not carried out in an effective manner because much of the agricultural practice is still on a subsistence level. The technical weaknesses of many of traditional agricultural systems can be blamed on the archaic customs and traditions that do not take into account the exploding populations in the developing countries. Population growth is exerting pressures on African natural resources.

The predominant traditional system of agriculture is shifting cultivation. There are several types of shifting cultivation, but the major characteristics can be summarized as follows:

1. Many farmlands are nonpermanent (i.e., abandoned).
2. Forests and savannas are cleared and burned.
3. The farmlands are left fallow for a certain period of time, with fallow periods becoming progressively shorter because of development and population pressures.
4. Fertilizers are not used.

5. Farmers are not organized into cooperatives as in Western nations.

6. The farms are purely subsistence-level farms and are plagued by low production.

7. There is a lack of permanent capital (Okigbo 1980).

In order to appreciate the problems associated with shifting cultivation, it is pertinent in this research to give a thorough assessment of shifting cultivation in the African biomes. In the dense woody forests of the Guinean Zone, the farming system is shifting cultivation, which destroys the primary and secondary forests. In this region, there is a delicately balanced biological system between the soil and the vegetation. Fallen leaves from the trees provide an excellent breeding ground for microorganisms that accelerate the formation of humus. This topsoil (humus) is thin and covers deeper, infertile soil. The practice of shifting cultivation in the Guinean Zone, Equatorial Guinea, and the highlands and coastal regions of Africa exposes the humus to heavy rainfalls and high temperatures that lead to leaching and erosion (Walter 1973). These problems surface because shifting cultivation involves clearing and burning of vegetation and cutting down trees within forest zones and at the outskirts of the zones. In making one acre of farmland available, it is estimated that about 600,000 kilograms of timber is destroyed by shifting cultivation practices (FAO 1980).

In the light woodlands of the Guinean and the Guinean Equatorial Zones, shifting cultivation requires the cutting and burning of trees and vegetation from many acres of land to provide ashes to fertilize a small portion of the cleared forest. In some areas of the developing world, the roots of trees are removed from the ground by rudimentary methods of hoeing. Such action only enhances the process of soil erosion and loss of fertility by the soil.

In the drier savannas there are fewer deep-rooted trees and the humus (topsoil), although rich, is very thin. In this region, a much smaller area than those of Guinea and Equatorial Guinea is able to be fertilized through the cutting and burning of trees and vegetation. The common characteristic of shifting cultivation in all the regions of Africa is fallow periods during which the soil can regain some fertility. The main objectives of cutting and burning are to rid the farmland of plant residue while at the same time releasing nourishment in the form of phosphorus, potassium, and calcium to the soil. Such nutrients are essential to the grass that will eventually be used in feeding the livestock. The process of cutting and burning also destroys undesirable weeds and insects.

There is a tremendous loss of nitrogen, however, and it is argued by some researchers that the destruction of flora, fauna, and soil structure in several parts of northwest Africa have led to increased desertification

(FAO 1980). The pH of the soil increases due to the rise in temperature, and the burning destroys the nitrogen-fixing bacteria that are essential in the nitrogen cycle. Numerous microorganisms and mircofauna make the forest floor, which contains litter, their homes. Burning destroys these essential parts of the ecosystem. When soil is exposed because of the removal of its protective cover of vegetation, sheet erosion occurs after a heavy downpour.

The widespread clearing and burning of forest and the lack of proper management of farmlands by multinationals and natives pose serious threats to the biological systems in developing countries. The forests of Africa, like those of South America and Asia, evolved over millions of years but could be destroyed in a few decades. The signs are already prevalent in several countries in Africa. The possibility for a natural regrowth of trees in Africa is almost nil at this stage, unless the threat from expanding population is curbed. The abandonment of land is supposed to enhance the soil's ability to regain some of its fertility, but in the long run, the soil under the shifting cultivation method eventually loses almost all of its fertility and the land becomes useless.

Other traditional African agricultural methods worth mention are practiced in the Sudan belt and in northern Africa. Figure 8 shows a schematic diagram of one such agricultural system. Within a certain land boundary the village is centrally located. In a ring fashion, dwellings are found surrounded by gardens that provide vegetables for the village inhabitants. Away from the dwellings are the first set of fields (f1), which maintain a certain level of fertility because domestic refuse and cattle waste are dumped on them. These fields are cultivated regularly and also left fallow. At some distance away from the first set of fields is another set (f2). These are never fertilized or manured but are cultivated or left fallow. The problem with this agricultural practice is the increase in the village population. The fallow periods are becoming shorter and the soil fertility is rapidly decreasing as more and more land is needed for human habitation.

In West Africa, the Serer people practice an indigenous agricultural system in which the farmers not only engage in crop farming but also raise livestock that provide manure for the soil. A similar practice can be seen further north in Morocco, Algeria, and parts of Libya. In these countries, animals such as camels, which can withstand drought, are used for plowing and preparing the land for cultivation.

The nomadic agricultural system is worth special mention in this study precisely because of the problems it generates. Figure 9 shows the areas of Africa where animal husbandry is practiced. The idea of being confined to one area is considered by the nomads to be an impediment to their success as farmers. The nomads move from place to place in order to find good grazing vegetation. The concept of migration and free range has

Figure 8
Fallow Cultivation

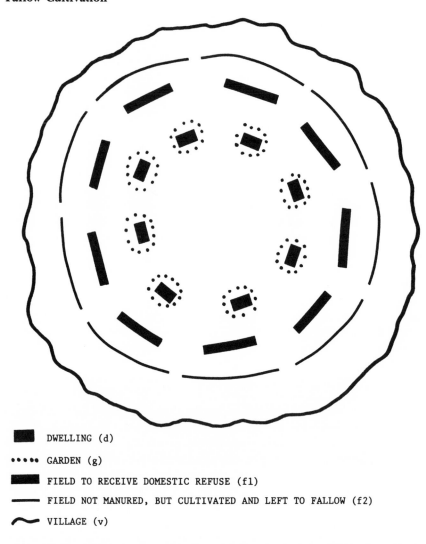

■ DWELLING (d)

•••• GARDEN (g)

▧ FIELD TO RECEIVE DOMESTIC REFUSE (f1)

— FIELD NOT MANURED, BUT CULTIVATED AND LEFT TO FALLOW (f2)

〜 VILLAGE (v)

devastating environmental repercussions. In northern Nigeria, for example, there is a deliberate burning of grazing grounds so that much health-
ier grass can grow in place of the forest. As was pointed out earlier, the
nomadic movement is in a north-to-south direction, and the burning is
usually done before departing in search of other grazing ground. One
could draw a generalization that the pastoral lifestyle of the nomads is one
of the agents of the steady decrease in African forestland.

In the developing countries of Africa, it is imperative that farmers un-

Figure 9
Animal Husbandry in Africa

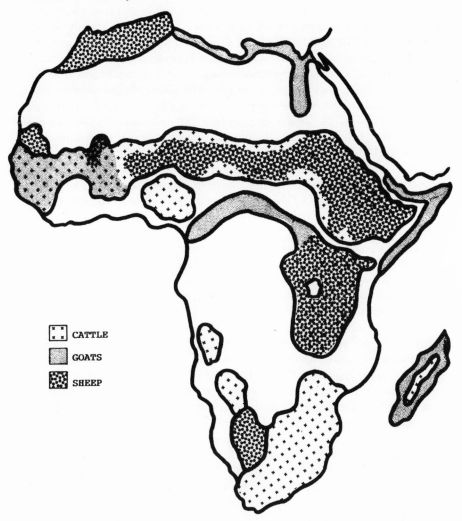

CATTLE

GOATS

SHEEP

derstand the equilibrium of the savannas and forests. The disruption of ecological equilibrium in many nations of Africa occurs mainly because the natural resources are used without sufficient consideration for the balance in the biomes. In the rainy season, the grass of the savanna flourishes. When the grass is used for grazing purposes, the soil is left with excess water. The woody plants, such as acacia species, find room to develop in great numbers. They produce fruit and seeds that are subsequently dispersed by animals, wind, and insects in livestock dung. The acacia seeds develop into thorny shrubs that are completely useless to livestock. This type of condition leads to brush encroachment resulting in man-made deserts (DeSanto 1978). Figure 10 is a schematic explanation of what could happen in a grassland as a result of livestock grazing. There is no doubt that in Africa, the combined defoliation by nomadic herds, village animals, and shifting cultivation has accelerated the decline in soil fertility.

The people of developing nations, especially in Africa and South America, have traditionally engaged in hunting and fishing for subsistence consumption. In the past, wild animals and fish have been major parts of their diets, but data on the animal population, for example, the African elephant, indicate that native animal populations have drastically declined.

Some well-planned field investigations in countries like Kenya, Uganda, and Tanzania have shown that commercial hunting and fishing without proper and adequate management have done great damage to the fish and animal populations of those countries. The commercial exploitation of fish and animals is a threat to the world biological system.

It was pointed out earlier that most small-scale farming operations are embarked upon solely for subsistence. It should, however, be pointed out that forest farming, which is mostly subsistence agriculture, always follows commercial logging. Commercial logging has been intensified in recent times (1980 to 1990) by many African countries, such as Ghana and Nigeria. These countries have increased their logging activities because they are heavily indebted to foreign banks and have to pay the interests on their loans. With the assistance of multinationals, in some cases, they exploit their forests—thus destroying the homes of thousands of plants and animals. When the logging is finished, a large number of farmers take advantage of the cleared land. Subsistence agriculture is not a problem when practiced by a small number of people, but when the number of farmers exceeds the carrying capacity of the land, environmental problems result. The small-scale farmers cultivate the land continously—year after year—without the fallow periods necessary for the land to regain some of its fertility. Southeast Asia is a good example of a region of the developing world where forest farming has caused serious damage to the ecosystem.

STATISTICAL EVIDENCE

Having discussed the major traditional systems of farming in Africa and having critically examined the problems associated with these systems, it is worthwhile to substantiate the argument made in this chapter with statistical data that support the arguments. The most appropriate point of departure is to examine the population data. Between 1970 and 1982, all the countries shown in Table 2 had population increases. The percentage of people actively involved in agriculture has steadily declined in all the African countries. This generalization holds true for all developing countries

Figure 10
Progressive Destruction of a Savanna Region

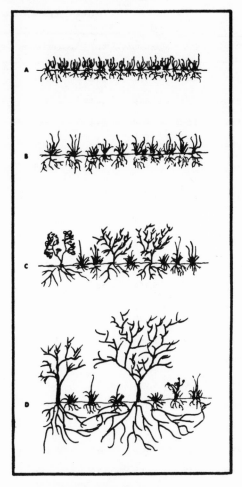

A = Flourishing grassland
B = Reduction of grass
C = Beginning of thorny woody plants
D = Full blown thorny plants

of the world. Although the number of people farming the land has increased, the total population has increased at a much faster rate, and since the agriculture is predominantly unmechanized, food production is low. As was pointed out earlier, cash crop production and migration of young people to urban centers exacerbate the problem of food production.

Revelle (1976) and Brown (1978) argue that two centuries ago, most of the world's energy supply came from traditional sources such as wood.

Table 2
Population Data of Selected African Countries (in thousands)

COUNTRY	YEAR	POPULATION TOTAL	POPULATION AGRICULTURAL	ECONOMICALLY ACTIVE POPULATION TOTAL	ECONOMICALLY ACTIVE POPULATION IN AGRICULTURE	ECONOMICALLY ACTIVE POPULATION PERCENT IN AGRICULTURE
GAMBIA	1970	449	368	234	191	81.9
	1975	524	419	263	211	80.0
	1980	603	470	294	229	78.0
	1981	619	480	300	233	77.5
	1982	635	490	300	230	77.1
GHANA	1970	8,614	5,075	3,346	1,955	58.4
	1975	9,990	5,507	3,754	2,051	54.6
	1980	11,679	5,988	4,327	2,197	50.8
	1981	12,063	6,089	4,453	2,226	50.0
	1982	12,462	6,192	4,584	2,255	49.2
GUINEA	1970	3,921	3,320	1,870	1,583	84.7
	1975	4,416	3,644	2,037	1,681	82.5
	1980	5,014	4,019	2,237	1,793	80.1
	1981	5,147	4,098	2,282	1,816	79.6
	1982	5,285	4,180	2,328	1,841	79.1
GUIN BISSAU	1970	487	424	150	137	87.0
	1975	527	447	166	141	84.8
	1980	573	471	176	144	82.2
	1981	583	476	178	145	81.6
	1982	594	481	180	146	81.0
IVORY COAST	1970	5,341	4,513	2,851	2,409	84.5
	1975	6,760	5,547	3,491	2,865	82.1
	1980	8,034	6,374	4,015	3,185	79.3
	1981	8,298	6,532	4,121	3,244	78.7
	1982	8,568	6,693	4,228	3,303	78.1

Source: Food and Agriculture Organization. 1982. *FAO Production Yearbook*. Vol. 36. Rome: FAO. p. 62.

The situation has changed for many Western nations. On the other hand, the situation for many developing countries is still the same as it was two centuries ago because noncommercial energy is derived from wood (Binzangi 1985). The continued dependence on wood as a major source of energy for domestic usage in many African countries poses a great threat to the timber and the forest at large. Deforestation and the process of desertification will continue unless drastic measures are taken to slow down the pace at which natural resources are being destroyed.

As was mentioned earlier, shifting cultivation is one of the primary causes of forest destruction. It is practiced in most African countries and is based on the fallow method. In the savanna region of Africa, many of the countries that have resorted to "operation feed the nation" have experienced indiscriminate destruction of their forest land. In all developing countries of the world, there is an increasing demand for wood for domestic and industrial purposes, and wood is exported for foreign exchange. The pace of consumption has increased exponentially as population increases at the same rate. Unfortunately, the supply cannot keep up with the pace of demand. This situation has led to the deficit problem in many developing nations.

Data published by the FAO (1981) indicate that fuel wood production represented about 5.4 percent of the energy consumption in the world a decade ago. That percentage increased in the 1980s. In Africa, it has been estimated that over 97 percent of the energy requirement in rural areas is supplied by fuel wood.

The threat to the forest and savanna ecosystems comes from nomadic pastoralism, farming methods (shifting), and timber lumbering. These three practices must be managed properly; otherwise desertification cannot be stopped. Desertification involves ecological changes that deprive the land of its ability to sustain agriculture and human habitation. In the 1970s, land degradation in the southern part of the Sahara made news all over the world. In the 1980s there was degradation in the northern parts of the Sahara. The production capacity of land in countries such as Morocco, Algeria, Tunisia, and Libya is falling. As a result of the unwise use of land in countries such as Botswana, Kenya, Tanzania, and Ethiopia, these countries are facing serious desertification problems. It must be recapitulated that problems will be worse in the year 2000 if the growing populations in African countries are not checked.

Ethiopia used to be a forested nation, with about 40 percent of the country under high forestation. Today, that country has less than 4 percent forest (FAO 1983). Many decades of shifting and pastoral agricultural practices have led to the catastrophes that were broadcast on the daily news in the Western countries in the 1980s. Exploitation of this kind can be seen all over Africa.

Gander (1984) notes that in many developing countries, the concentration of people in large urban centers has led to the demand for organic combustible materials. Consequently, the wood entrepreneurs have devised dangerous methods of obtaining wood without regard to the ecological implications. Reforestation is still in its elementary stages in many parts of the developing world. For example, only as recently as two decades ago has the federal government of Nigeria, with the assistance of international organizations, begun reforestation in northern Nigeria.

FURTHER CONSEQUENCES OF FOREST CLEARANCE

The traditional agricultural system of shifting cultivation was once a good method of farming, but with increasing populations, development of cities, and other aspects of modernization, this method of farming is not providing an answer to the agricultural problems of many emerging nations. The elimination of virgin forests through traditional agricultural practices and commercial logging has the capability of affecting local, regional, and global climates. Henderson-Sellers (1981:443) notes:

The changes caused to the environment which are believed to be of significance for the climate are: (i) increased surface albedo; (ii) perturbation of the carbon cycle causing variations in the atmospheric levels of CO_2; (iii) local changes in the water balance; (iv) addition of particulates to the troposphere, both directly from combustion and by increasing the wind-blown dust, and (v) pertubation of the hydrological and turbulence characteristics over areas where tall forest stands are replaced by low crops or cleared land.

Deforestation caused by inappropriate agricultural practices also leads to sedimentation of water reservoirs and hydropower installations.

WOMEN'S IMPACT ON TRADITIONAL AND MODERN AGRICULTURAL SYSTEMS IN AFRICA

Planning for the overall development of Third World countries demands that policymakers, educators, and citizens understand the importance of a systems approach to problem solving. The problems of developing countries are multifaceted as far as development is concerned.

One of the major elements of the solution to the development problems of Third World nations is agriculture. Agriculture has the most important place in the development of Africa, but many of the leaders and policymakers do not put enough emphasis on this important element of development, as Carl Eicher (1986:5) notes:

The historical record reveals that heads of African states and donors have seriously misunderstood both the role of agriculture in national development at this stage of Africa's economic history and the strategic importance of a reliable agricultural surplus as a precondition for the expansion of the industrial sector.

History has shown that women's work in Africa has always been critical in the stability of the family and the community as a whole. It should be pointed out that the role of women is not the same all across Africa.

The Origin of Women's Impact

During the period when African society was based on hunting-gathering, the roles of women and men were very distinct. The men hunted, while the women and children gathered the vegetable crops from the forest, which at the time was very generous. At that time, the carrying capacity of Africa's natural resources had not been exceeded, as is the case in many parts of Africa today. With increasing population due, in part, to the polygamous family system, it was necessary to sow crops. This was done by clearing small parcels of forest for agricultural purposes. It should be pointed out that this type of agricultural system is still being practiced in the rural areas of Africa today (Boserup 1970).

The era of colonization opened up Africa to many Western influences, among which was the utilization of underemployed men. Europeans set up plantations in order to produce crops that were useful in factories and industries in Europe. For example, many Yoruba men in Nigeria were employed in cocoa and timber plantations; Annang and Efik men were employed in palm product plantations. Thus, cash crop production was one area where men's labor was concentrated. African men became interested in earning an income in order to purchase European-made goods. This pattern is certainly one of the reasons for the deterioration of a social economy; it marks the beginning of the breakdown of a previously self-sufficient society. The African economy became linked to the Western money-based economy and thereby dependent on the industrialized countries for goods and products.

While African men were working for the colonialists, African women continued their subsistence agriculture in order to maintain the family, which included children and older members of the family who could not fend for themselves. Their role was instrumental in sustaining the African family.

The discovery of minerals and oil in countries like Nigeria, Ghana, Zaire, and Cameroon also exacerbated the problem of men having to leave their homes and increasing the work load of women in agriculture. Men could earn more income by working in the mines than by farming, and as a result many of them left their rural communities.

The Roles of Women in Traditional and Modern Farming Systems

The African traditional farms are small in size in comparison with the modern farms. The Food and Agriculture Organization (FAO) in 1971 estimated a size of about thirteen acres or less. Crops such as vegetables, yams, cocoyams, sweet potatoes, maize, plantains, and bananas are grown. These farms can be found in the rural parts of Africa. The majority of African traditional farmers are women who use the hoe as their primary tool. In the "hoe culture" system, Baumann (1928) observes that men clear the bush for the women who work on the farms. The Annang, Efik, and Ebibio people of Nigeria still practice this type of agricultural system.

The colonial era in Africa will be remembered for influencing the departure of men from their traditional roles and increasing the women's responsibility as major providers and heads of many homes. It could also be said that the colonial era set the stage for the breakup of the African family and society. Young men left their wives and children behind in search of work on plantations and mines. In some cases, the women went with their husbands to assist them in their jobs. Such transitions disrupted the traditional lifestyles in the rural communities. The stagnation of food production, coupled with an exponential population explosion, brought hardship to many rural communities. The trend of youth migration away from agricultural communities has continued in modern-day Africa and has perpetuated the problem of scarcity of foodstuff. This trend of social migration disrupted the natural flow of inculcated knowledge of agricultural practice from one generation to the next. Hence, the resultant responsibility of women in agricultural production and the need to support their roles as farmers. According to Pala (1976:2), rural development is supposed to accomplish the following goals:

1. To increase per capita output and market orientation among the rural population.

2. To increase food production commensurate with the rapid population growth.

3. To insure equitable redistribution of aggregate income.

4. To reduce regional inequalities in per capita income.

5. To reduce the rate of rural-urban migration.

6. To gain a precise and scientific understanding of the social and ecological environment in which rural change is to occur.

With regard to the expectations of rural development, women's role is significant because their success on the farms affects rural farm families. For instance, the famine situation in many parts of Africa, although greatly influenced by environmental factors, was also affected by the failure of agricultural output due to disruptive Western influences on the African traditional system of crop production.

The hoe agricultural system that predominated during the colonial era was known for its long fallow periods. The women had long working days, and in parts of Africa where this type of agriculture is still being practiced, the working days for women are still very long. Boserup (1970:12) concludes that during the colonial era, men spent an average of fourteen hours per week on agricultural work, while women spent fifteen hours. In addition to the agricultural work, they continued their roles as mothers and performed household chores such as cooking and cleaning, working well into the night.

The African colonial era saw women working side by side with men in the production of crops. Unfortunately, in this relationship women were unpaid partners. The women continued with their subsistence crop production while also assisting their spouses with the cash crop production (Boserup 1970).

With the end of the colonial era, women's agricultural contribution increased due to the geometric growth in population and migration from rural to urban centers. In other words, the problems of the postcolonial era actually began in the colonial era. The colonial rulers did a poor job of planning for the postcolonial years. They were more interested in dividing Africa into countries and subdividing the countries into regions in order to exploit the natural resources and rule the people. As a matter of fact, they accentuated the differences in the linguistic groups, creating a social imbalance among peoples who had previously lived harmoniously.

The urban centers were not capable of absorbing the new migrant populations from the rural areas. Cities such as Lagos, Ibadan, Onitsha, Abeokuta, Enugu, and Benin in Nigeria were and still are seriously overcrowded. With decreasing agricultural production and increasing urbanization, there was urgent demand for locally produced food. Given this scenario, women's agricultural production was incapable of supplying all the needed food. Thus, the importation of food increased tremendously at the end of the colonial era in order to keep pace with demand, benefiting the more developed countries and increasing the dependency of Africa on the industrialized world.

Countries like Nigeria once produced approximately 95 percent of its food crops but now import about 80 percent of their food from foreign countries. This imbalance further has worsened the economic situation. Thus, one could conclude that colonialism led to multiple problems in Africa today. While the countries of Africa continue to plunge into debt, the industrialized countries seem to be exacerbating the worsening situation while benefiting from an unequal exchange of resources. For example, imported agricultural technology that is inappropriately suited to the climate and terrain of African countries does little to increase the food production of the continent. The exchange of Western technology for nonrenewable and renewable natural resources further depletes the continent of its wealth.

There have always been arguments about women's position in African development. There are two schools of thought on the issue:

One school of thought sees women's role in African development as a subservient one. Pala (1976) argued that this viewpoint is the one advanced by Europeans. Women's contributions are seen as being secondary to whatever men do. The women do not receive the recognition that they deserve. They are thought of as receiving directions and orders from the men while they (the women) do the hoeing, weeding, tending vegetables, food production (preparation), and child rearing. It is possible for this opinion to be held by Europeans because women's role in Western countries is culturally different from those in Africa. Pala (1976) mentioned that as far back as 1932, Driberg attempted to discuss this myth of the subservient role of African women. It was suggested that more rigorous studies should be conducted to investigate the division of labor between men and women in Africa.

The opposing school of thought contends that women's roles are complementary to those of men. It is argued that when one takes into consideration the progress from precolonial Africa to the postcolonial days, it could be seen that women's roles have been increasing in importance. This recognition by the governments of African countries such as Ghana, Nigeria, Sierra Leone, and Zaire has meant that women's ideas are beginning to be seriously considered during the planning phases of agricultural development. Such steps have led to improvement in subsistence agricultural production. The significance of women's role is increasingly recognized, and donor countries and African countries are providing substantial assistance to enhance the development of rural women in agricultural production.

In the past, donor countries did not understand the importance of women's role in rural agricultural development in Africa and as a result dealt only with men when attempting to provide assistance for agricultural and other developments. Fortunately, this attitude is changing; there is a shift in emphasis to the encouragement of rural women. Presvelou (1980:106) argues that efforts to support rural women should ensure the following:

—that careful attention be given to the repercussions of each project on rural women;

—that the advancement of women's cause not be impaired, that women benefit as much as men from the ongoing programs, and that such programs include no ideological clauses likely to reduce the contribution of the African, Asiatic, or Latin American rural woman in the development of her country:

—that women and girls play a role in overall national programming by being involved in the selection, operationalization, implementation, and evaluation of projects affecting them:

—that the contributions of rural women in the national economy be explicitly recognized;

—finally, that the participation of women be encouraged in each and every initiative intended to improve the development of their countries.

Another hindrance to agricultural development in Africa is the land tenure system. Traditionally, in most African societies, women do not inherit land from their fathers. Hence, only a small fraction of agricultural land belongs to women. This is an area in which the African government can assist women. In Ikot Ekepene (in Akwa Ibom State of Nigeria), government land is partitioned and leased out to women at minimal fees for the purpose of raising crops. This strategy has increased crop production in the township, enabling the women to sell excess crops to neighbors and friends. In this community women may exchange ripened vegetables with neighboring women farmers, thereby increasing variety and yield. This attitude of sharing enforces friendly neighborliness, which benefits all community members.

Women also play a part in making sure that the pastoral activities succeed. Owning cattle, camels, and goats is considered a status enhancer in some parts of Africa. Three types of pastoral economies can be found in Africa (Pala 1976). One pastoral economy consists of a permanent homestead and a complementary dry season camp. The permanent homestead consists of a woman, her children, and older members of the extended family system. Examples can be found in Uganda and Sudan. Another type of pastoral economy involves meager grazing, in which browsing facilities determine livestock movement, as for example among the Turkina of Kenya (Pala 1976).

The Hausas and Fulanis of Nigeria who live in highland areas like Jos Plateau essentially divide their society into two. The lowland community raises cattle and the highland community grows the crops. The women maintain the agriculture on the highlands.

The precolonial, colonial, and postcolonial eras have all witnessed unpaid cooperative assistance within family, village, and linguistic groups in agriculture. In order to ensure agricultural productivity in the rural areas, men married several wives to provide large families to assist in farm production.

As a result of the introduction of cash crops and new technologies, production, and consumption patterns have changed. The commercialization of subsistence economy has lessened cooperation within the extended family. Women are getting paid more for their excess farm produce.

The introduction of Western-style techniques of marketing farm produce is destroying the traditional cooperation within the African village. Urban migration also exacerbates the problem of decreasing cooperation within the village. Nonetheless, it must be said that women's role in the social and economic development of Africa is gradually being recognized and appreciated. Women are being rewarded for their contributions to the small progress that African countries are making. Western women have assisted in uplifting the spirits and aspirations of African women, although it should be emphasized that many educated African women do not see the necessity for a Western-style women's movement.

There is no doubt that the more assistance that rural women receive from donor countries and African governments, the more improved the agricultural systems (semiintensive, permanent field, intensive traditional, and agro-pastoral) will become. The encouragement of African traditional agricultural systems will also assist in the preservation of the biological diversity of the continent.

HAZARDOUS WASTES IN AFRICA

The artificial division of Africa into countries by the European colonialists not only created a dependency situation, but it also exacerbated conflicts between African groups or countries. It resulted in modern African involvement in an arms race it cannot afford. Olowo (1989) estimates that about $230 billion is spent by African countries in the purchase of arms. This amount represents about 20 percent of Africa's debt burden.

During precolonial days, African people experienced conflicts but they were not of the magnitude of present-day conflicts. Mistrust and unnecessary competition among Africans has been encouraged by European and U.S. businesspeople who are more interested in selling their arms. The monies spent on the purchase of arms could be better spent on development projects. The benefit to Africans would encourage regional development and economic progress in the continent. The arms race fosters dependency on Western technology for the wrong purposes (Olowo 1989).

An emerging concern for many African countries as the world moves closer to the year 2000 is the management of hazardous wastes produced by the few industries that operate within the continent and the waste that is brought into Africa from foreign countries. Africa is gradually being envisaged as a possible place to dump waste from Europe and the United States. Faced with terrible economic problems, policymakers and some criminal citizens/government officials are allowing places in Africa to be used as dump sites for toxic substances.

Hazardous waste constitutes all substances that can cause harmful impacts to living organisms and the environment at large if not properly managed and controlled. Given the fact that many African nations have just established ministries of environment within the last decade or do not have departments that deal with environmental problems, the dumping of hazardous wastes in Africa would be very disastrous. Environmental awareness and studies are still in their infancies in many parts of Africa. The majority of the citizens are not familiar with the ramifications of the hazardous substances. To indicate the gravity of the problem, Table 3 lists African countries that are engaged in the importation of hazardous waste. The threat of these hazardous wastes to the ecological systems of Africa should be understood by African governments. Once the hazardous wastes arrive, they are not properly handled. The inhabitants of the areas close to the dump sites are not informed about what is being buried close to their homes or in their villages. Their children play with drums containing the hazardous wastes, and the women farm close to the sites. The long-term effects, which include cancer, malformation of unborn children, and other chronic and acute diseases, far outweigh the money that is paid to the governments. In addition, the European and U.S. companies that are involved indulge in other illegal practices, such as corrupting the native population of villages where the dumping takes place. For example, community leaders and citizens of Koko, Nigeria were bribed into dumping hazardous waste.

It is estimated that the waste disposal business generates about $12 billion a year and that 300 million tons of toxic wastes are produced by only 24 industrialized nations (Ayadike 1988). The lifestyles in the industrialized countries produce exorbitant waste, which must be put somewhere. Recently, people in many Western countries have come to the realization that they are gradually running out of places to dump the waste. Many Western citizens are also demanding environmentally safe communities in which to raise their children and live their lives without having to worry about contaminated environments.

Events in the United States in the past five years have shown how sensitive communities are about wastes from other states. In 1988, a barge traveled up and down the eastern seaboard of the United States and the Gulf of Mexico looking for a place to dump its load of solid waste. In 1989, a train loaded with sludge traveled the United States looking for a state that would accept it for a price. It went back to the state where it originated. Given these trends, the developing countries have become more attractive as dumping sites to companies wanting to dispose of their wastes. Unfortunately, the dire economic situation in African countries encourages the acceptance of the waste.

However, governments such as Nigeria have become alert to the toxic waste problem and have instituted drastic laws against acts of "toxic terror-

Table 3
The African Dumping Sites: African Countries Actively Importing Wastes (according to Greenpeace)

BENIN

Nonnuclear industrial waste from North America and Europe

Volume: 1 million to 5 million tons per year

Method of disposal: "Recycling plant to be built after 2–3 years"

Under a contract dated January 1988 the exporter, Sesco Ltd. of Gibraltar, will deliver up to 5 million tons each year and will pay Benin $2.50 per ton of waste delivered.

Radioactive waste from France

Volume: two shiploads

Method of disposal: landfill

According to *Africa Analysis*, April 1988, President Kerekou has "decided that waste will be buried on the outskirts of Abomey . . . one of centres of opposition to Kerekou." The site has reportedly now been changed to the lake Aheme region close to the Togo border.

CONGO

Solvent, paint, pesticide sludge, and chemical wastes from the United States and Europe.

Volume: 1 million tons between June 1988 and May 1989

In April, the U.S. embassy in Brazzaville announced that the government of Congo had agreed to take 1 million tons of industrial waste over a 12-month period but in May, the Congo reportedly retracted this agreement, with the information minister, Chistaina Gilbert-Bembet, saying: "The Congo would rather stay poor but dignified."

EQUATORIAL GUINEA

Mixed chemical wastes from Europe

Volume: 2 million drums

Method of disposal: landfill on Annobon Island

African Analysis reports that a British firm has a 10-year license to dispose of 10 million drums of waste in exchange for payment of $1.6 million.

GABON

Uranium mining wastes from Colorado, USA

Volume and method of disposal: not available

According to *West African Hotline*, President Bongo met with the board of Denison Mining of Colorado in 1987 and agreed to take unspecified quantities of uranium tailing wastes.

Table 3 (continued)

GUINEA

Garbage and incinerator ash from Philadelphia, USA, and Norway

Volume: 15,000 tons

Method of disposal: dumped on Dassa Island, off Conakry

After receiving reports of the toxicity of the ash from Greenpeace, the government of Guinea is attempting to force the shippers, Bulkhandling, to remove the ash, and may have detained two of the company's staff to help speed the removal.

GUINEA-BISSAU

Industrial, pharmaceutical, and other waste from the United Kingdom, Switzerland, and the United States

Volume: 1 million–3.5 million tons per year, 15 million tons over five years

Method of disposal: landfill and possible incineration

It is reported that waste is to be dumped on land owned by Carlos Bernard Vieira, brother of the president, although the government has apparently not yet given final consent. Another separate possibility is that a landfill site will be established on an island off Guinea-Bissau, but "any proposals will not be forthcoming for at least 3–4 months."

NIGERIA

Chemical and industrial wastes, including those containing PCB, from Italy

Volume: 5,800 tons

Method of disposal: dumping near Koko port, Bendel State

SENEGAL

Type of waste not specified

Volume: not available

Method of disposal: a site 40 kilometers north of Dakar

A Swiss company, Intercontrat SA, is reported to be negotiating a contract with Sodilo of Senegal for use of the disposal site.

SOUTH AFRICA

Mercury-laced sludge wastes from New Jersey, United States

Volume: 2 shipments of 60 drums each per year

Method of disposal: to be recycled and the mercury reclaimed

Two shipments were made in 1986, but it is not clear whether South Africa has agreed to take any more shipments.

Table 3 (continued)

ZIMBABWE

Hazardous waste from armed forces agencies in the United States

Volume: at least 1,500 gallons

Method of disposal: dumping in phosphate mine pit

Exported from the United States by Jack and Charles Colbert, sentenced in February 1988 to 13 years' imprisonment for fraudulent business practices. Two hundred and seventy-five drums, falsely labeled as cleaning fluids, were purchased by a company in Zimbabwe with federal funds from the U.S. Agency for International Development.

Source: Ayadike, Obinna. 1988. "Toxic Terrorism." *West Africa* (June 20): 1108.

ism." It must be pointed out that educating citizens on environmental issues is the most effective means of combating this problem.

In tackling the problem of toxic waste importation, African governments must cooperate with one another. This recommendation is given in light of the recent events in Morocco and Sierra Leone. In these two countries, there were secret plans to construct toxic disposal plants to handle European and American wastes. The exposure of the project led to the discontinuation of the proposed construction.

The alarming issue is that African countries are being enticed by Western monies mainly to offset the debt they owe to Western banks. Such temptations would have long-term catastrophic environmental impacts. Many of the government officials who engage in the negotiations are misinformed about the environmental impact of the wastes. Fortunately, the Organization for African Unity (OAU) is now actively involved in monitoring any negotiations on the construction of plants or the importing of waste. This will discourage potential importers of wastes from industrialized countries.

Another problem is the dumping of unwanted or banned products from industrialized countries in Africa. For example, banned or outdated medicines or drugs are sold on the streets of many African countries, and chemists and pharmacies in many developing nations sell outdated medicines. This activity has led to the deaths of thousands of people and has harmed many unborn babies. Infant milk formulas that are not properly prepared are sold to unsuspecting African women who feed their children with the products that are claimed to be better than breast milk (with no factual basis). The children suffer from a number of problems such as diarrhea and other complications as a result of being fed such an infant formula. Their parents are unaware that breast milk is much better than baby formula because it contains the nutrients necessary for development and is especially beneficial to the immune system of the infant.

CONCLUSIONS AND RECOMMENDATIONS

One purpose of this chapter has been to merge the piecemeal efforts of other researchers concerning the environmental consequences of natural resource abuse in developing countries. Farmers in developing countries must cease cutting down and burning large acres of land. Instead, plots should be cleared in small areas that are bordered by forest fallows. This is beneficial because the fallows will inhibit erosion.

As stated earlier, several areas of the developing countries have been denuded of forest. A recent publication of *West Africa* (1989:2008) illustrates the seriousness of the problem of forest destruction in Africa—specifically in Nigeria:

Nonetheless, the obvious finiteness of forests, the fact that it does not stretch the memory to remember the trees where now there is scrub and dust, that destruction can reach rates of five per cent per year, that until recently Nigeria was a timber exporter but today spends $160m per year on imports, has lent urgency to debate. The international community has produced the Tropical Forest Action Plan framework, calling for expenditure of $5.32bn in the period 1987–91, while other FAO estimates suggest the need to invest $13–17bn per year to foster forestry development. In the last few years, any number of trees have been felled to feed the presses publishing treatises from timber producers and processors, consumers, and campaigners. Although a pittance against the finance needed to achieve significant results, donor money is beginning to flow towards forest projects, increasing by 65 percent in 1984–88 to around $1bn per year—not that everyone views this growth uncritically.

The practice of multiple cropping can enable the land to retain much of its fertility and enhances soil cover during the rainy season. The use of fire in destroying unwanted plants and animals certainly has its merits, but the demerits outweigh the benefits. Hence the use of fire should be moderated and used very carefully and selectively. The timing of fire in pasture management is crucial. Experts recommend the use of fire only during the day.

In order to reverse the ongoing trend of grassland, savanna, and forest destruction in developing countries, several steps will have to be taken by the citizens (farmers) and the governments of developing nations:

1. Alternative sources of energy should be sought. Fortunately this has already started in the wealthier developing nations, such as Nigeria, Gabon, Senegal, and other Third World oil-producing nations.

2. People's attitudes will have to be influenced through education so that farmers can practice subsistence agriculture more wisely through the use of fertilizers. The use of fertilizers must be monitored by appropriate agencies and departments, because fertilizers, when not properly used, can contaminate

drinking water and destroy ponds, lakes, and rivers. They build up in the food chain and can cause health problems.

3. The importance of conservation cannot be understated when discussing the natural resources of developing nations. The governments of developing nations should have laws that prohibit unnecessary burning and cutting. Governments should acquire land for forest reserves.

4. Many developing countries, like Nigeria, have begun reforestation projects. Other countries should emulate this example.

5. The governments of developing nations must have local, regional, and national policies that encourage supervision of farmers so that they can set up cooperatives that would advance their interests and the interests of the nation. It is only when a balance is struck between preservation and use that the resources of the developing nations will be saved from total destruction.

6. Family planning must be emphasized to the people of the developing countries through education, incentives, and government.

No matter how the governments do in terms of restricting the use of resources, it is the education of the farmers and commercial entrepreneurs with regard to the ecological system (balance) that is the most important factor in preserving the resources. On the whole, future research and technological development may make it possible to improve food production in the developing countries. It is the opinion of the author that, based on the current trends as portrayed by the statistical data in this study, the future looks bleak for the natural resources of many developing nations. The solutions must begin with the desire of both the people and their governments to change the pattern for the better.

3 THE IMPACT OF TRANSNATIONALS AND MULTINATIONALS ON AFRICA

The literature on multinational corporations is filled with discussions of the positive and the negative impacts of transnational firms on the development of Third World countries.

The traditional neoclassical paradigm contends that foreign investment in developing countries offers the host countries hard currency (capital), technological hardware and skills, managerial skills, and marketing skills, improving the efficiency of operation, generating employment opportunities and accelerating competition (Moran 1985). Although Vernon (1986) has offered an explanation of why decisions are made by corporations to invest or operate abroad, that is, as a strategy to keep pace with the transfer of technology and managerial skills and thus take advantage of the low cost of production, opponents of the traditional neoclassical paradigm argue that such arrangements only continue the dependency that colonialism started.

Lall and Streeten (1977) argue that multinational corporations do not offer much in terms of new capital. They contend that these firms usually tap local capital in order to survive. Development of Third World nations is purposefully misinterpreted by multinationals in order to offer a distorted picture of development. Before examining tourism development as an example of how multinational corporations benefit more than do host countries, it is imperative to discuss the issues of the neoconventional paradigm with respect to multinationals.

The first issue is that investment by multinational corporations exacerbates conflict, which could be either domestic or international in scale.

For example, conflicts could develop between the multinationals and the host countries, resulting in the nationalization of the companies in the host countries. In order to be compensated for their losses, the multinational could ask for help from the World Bank and a long, drawn-out litigation would ensue. The host countries could perceive the investment as a form of dominance if they do not play significant roles.

Another area of concern is that the host countries experience a new outflow of capital, which does not promote a long-range development strategy. The profits that are generated by the businesses owned by transnational corporations in African countries do not remain within the boundaries of these countries to be reinvested in other projects. The outflow of capital caused by the actions of multinationals makes it difficult for African countries to have a decent balance of payment. Multinationals transfer excessive amounts of money overseas. This movement of capital creates a dependency that perpetuates inequalities. African and foreign financial institutions favor European and American firms because they appear to be more creditworthy. This type of arrangement makes it easier for the multinational firms to succeed.

A third problem created by multinationals for developing countries is that the exports from African countries are underpriced to favor industrialized nations, while imports are overpriced. This is a legacy of colonialism that continues to add difficulties to the development process of emerging African countries.

In order to attract multinationals, some African countries have created conditions that are providing a favorable competitive edge to the multinationals, yet some of the multinationals put forward conditions that make it impossible for the governments to benefit. For example, if the business ventures should fail, the African government incurs the burdens. In some cases, as Biersteker (1978:5) notes, there are "tie-in clauses similar to those associated with aid projects that require the subsidiary or licensee to purchase intermediate parts and capital goods from the parent corporation that supplied the basic technology."

It should also be pointed out that because the multinational firms have very few ties to the local economic system, they really have very little to lose if the business should fail because they are entities by themselves. For example, they do not have the local business contributing to their operational system. In other words, symbiotic relationships are not established with local businesses. Most of the supplies for the operation of multinationals are imported from abroad. Such a situation brings about the displacement of indigenous production and the transfer of inappropriate technology.

In order to examine some of the issues raised in the above discussion, let us explore the impact of tourism on some African countries.

THE IMPACT OF TOURISM ON THE ECONOMIES OF AFRICAN COUNTRIES

In the last two decades, policymakers, economists, and planners in Africa have focused their attention on the relationship between economic development and the exponential increase in the population of African nations. They have had to tackle the problem of delineating the cause and the effect of the geometric increase in population.

There is a great deal of debate in the literature on whether economic development accelerates or retards population growth rates (Todaro 1985). This section focuses on that gap in the economic development of Africa that tourism development can fill given the right incentives, leadership, commitment, education, and understanding of the potentials of the continent.

Research and development in the aviation industry revolutionized international tourism, which accounts for about 6 percent of world trade. Only a small fraction of that trade occurs in the continent of Africa. Travel and tourism researchers contend that visitor travel, worldwide, will rise from the current 300 million visits annually to 500 million by the year 2000 (Bale and Drakakis-Smith 1988). Countries endowed with natural resources could develop their resources in order to lure foreign visitors to the attractions. Such a strategy could enable Africa to share in the projected rise in tourism.

As an invisible industry, tourism in Africa as well as other parts of the world does not possess any tangible product. Most trips to Africa are transactions between travelers and foreign carriers. These carriers generally carry wealthy and middle-class foreign visitors to exotic and scenic parts of Africa. This type of arrangement makes tourism development in Africa very difficult.

Significant Aspects of International Tourism

There are several aspects of tourism that are germane to the issue of international tourism, but probably the most important ones in terms of economic ramifications are those that actually control the international market. Specialized market techniques now pervade the tourism industry and have transformed it into an organized business that operates just like any other transnational industry (Bale and Drakakis-Smith 1988).

In many Western countries such as the United States, Canada, Great Britain, West Germany, and France, rising incomes have enabled many people of these countries to seek exciting vacation spots in developing countries where their currencies enjoy enormous buying power because of the devaluation of currencies in the host countries. Increased mobility due to an improved aviation industry has made possible accessibility to many Third World countries of Africa. People from industrialized countries are in search of vacation places that differ from their home environments. They would like places that provide some form of escapism from their day-to-day lifestyles. The Third World vacation places provide recreational experiences that are unique, tranquil, and culturally uplifting to the visitors. The average traveler to Africa has a university education and desires exposure to other cultures and environments.

New marketing strategies also affect travel demands to African countries. In areas of the developed countries where radio, television, and newspapers carry advertisements about vacation spots in developing countries, tourism to destinations in these countries has been on the rise. More countries in Africa should advertise aggressively if they desire to get a share of the tourism industry.

The tourist industry has four basic intermediaries: travel agents, tour companies, hotel companies, and transport companies. In Africa, these intermediaries are influenced by foreign investors and management. The reason for this is twofold: First, African countries are supposedly faced with other problems of development, and as such their governments do not seriously consider investment in the tourism industry as an important part of their development, given their generally poor economic conditions. Second, the management skills that are necessary to deal with international tourists are very limited, and tourism development in Africa demands the training and education of the people of the host countries.

Travel destinations in Africa, as around the world, are influenced by historical connections. Many people of African heritage travel to Africa annually to visit relatives and friends or for recreational purposes. Other factors that influence travel destinations are accessibility, stability in terms of politics, economy, social tranquility, nature of tourist products, and finally the search for foreign exchange.

Tourism's Role in Development

A review of the literature on tourism's role in development indicates two opposing viewpoints. The first view is classified as the political economy approach, which assumes that tourism in Third World countries follows the pattern of colonialism and economic dependency of developing nations on developed nations of the world. The political economy view takes an in-depth look at the cause of problems associated with international tourism.

Scope of Tourism Planning in Africa

With the increasing number of affluent middle-class population in the developed countries and an increase in leisure time, people seek exotic vacation spots around the world. Africa—especially East Africa—offers some of the recreational experiences that are sought by many vacationers.

Tourism industry is affected by three main factors: hotel management, airlines, and tour companies. It is argued by proponents of the political economy approach that these three branches of tourism are dominated by transnationals (Bale and Drakakis-Smith 1988).

The transnational hotels, airlines, and tour companies have had some temporary success in a few African nations because of certain characteristics that they possess. Bale and Drakakis-Smith (1988:12) discuss four main features that make it easy for transnationals to establish themselves:

1. They seldom invest large amounts of their own capital in Third World countries but seek such funds from private and government sources locally, thus minimizing risk.
2. Associated infrastructures like new roads and power supplies are essential in resort development and are similarly funded through local sources or via foreign loans.
3. A viable visitor flow results from worldwide marketing campaigns.
4. Transnational corporations participate in the profits of their Third World hotels through management fees, limited direct investment, and various licensing, franchise, and service agreements.

Inequalities between developed countries and Third World countries exist within airline and tour companies management, which are dominated by foreign companies; few African countries actually benefit from the airline fares and tour companies. African countries lack enough viable national carriers that can compete with foreign carriers for passengers from advanced countries. For example, the Nigerian airline has had great difficulty attracting foreigners to travel with the carrier. The passengers are predominantly Nigerians or are Nigerian residents of Europe or the United States. An attempt by some East African nations to establish regional airlines to compete with foreign carriers failed because of cost of maintenance, political instability, and differences in ideology. European and American transnational tour companies have better marketing strategies and so benefit more than their African counterparts. The inequality arrangement between African countries and the transnational corporations involved in tourism has resulted in three important consequences (Britton 1981):

1. Tourist expenditures are retained by the transnational companies.
2. Only some isolated enclaves of African countries are visited by tourists. For example, in East Africa (Serengeti) and in the Ivory Coast (Abidjan) the tourists do not really experience the true culture of the area.
3. The tourists contribute to the decadence of the African destination.

The second viewpoint or paradigm of tourism's role in development is the "functional approach." It is basically an analytical way of assessing the impact of international tourism. It is argued that tourism has three basic components: (1) the dynamic phase, (2) the static phase, and (3) the consequential phase (Mathieson and Wall 1982). The dynamic phase encompasses round-trip travel. The static phase covers the stay at the Third World destination, and the consequential phase deals with the economic, physical, and social impacts of tourism on the Third World environment.

As opposed to the political economy approach, which emphasizes the exploitative character of the transnational companies, the functional approach pays a great deal of attention to the tourists' characteristics.

In many African countries, tourism is just beginning to emerge as a concept and a practical issue that can be investigated and encouraged because of its possible economic gains. It is the view of the proponents of the functional approach that tourism planning should be in the forefront of the economic development of the countries that intend to make international and domestic tourism an integral part of their development. Some African countries, agencies, and transnational corporations have begun to realize the importance of tourism planning in the overall economic development of their countries. Given the potential that some African countries have for tourism development, it is then the responsibility of the public and private sectors to coordinate their efforts to benefit from the opportunities.

Nevertheless, the issue of tourism development can be subdivided into two areas: The feasibility of a profit-making venture in tourism is a major stimulus for the private sector, while concern for other aspects of the economy and social problems are the top priorities of the government.

Basis for Tourism Planning

Most literature on tourism in Third World countries and specifically African indicates two types of impact: positive and negative.

There are three areas where the positive impact is felt: economic, social, and environmental. Tourism has been shown to generate employment in general. This smokeless industry has strong impacts on several aspects of the economy of the host countries, for example, in transportation, lodging, food services, and amusement. As shown in Table 4, the overall growth of the tourism industry in Africa has grown. Zambia had a large increase in the growth of tourism between 1975 and 1982. International tourism offers opportunities to earn foreign exchange and to create local jobs. Table 5 shows tourist arrivals in Zambia. The tourists' impact on Zambian economy might be small, but the towns that are close to the sites that tourists visit enjoy benefits—in the areas of hotel development, infra-

Table 4
Growth of Tourist Arrivals in Zambia (average annual change, percent per annum)

Region	1970-1980	1975-1982	1979-1984	1975
Zambia	6.4	12.7	19.1	22.7
Africa	9.4	3.8	4.0	5.0
World	5.7	3.8	2.3	4.1

Source: Husbands, Winston. 1989. "Social Status and Perception of Tourism in Zambia." *Annals of Tourism Research.* 16: 240.

Table 5
Tourist Arrivals in Zambia

Year	From Africa		From Europe		From Rest of World		Total
	Number	Share*	Number	Share*	Number	Share*	
1970	37,269	79.3	7,536	16.0	2,177	4.7	46,982
1975	26,884	52.0	13,252	25.6	11,544	22.4	51,680
1978	35,129	65.9	12,568	23.6	5,630	11.5	53,327
1979	31,022	57.6	15,179	28.2	7,684	14.2	53,885
1980	64,816	74.6	14,918	17.2	7,197	8.2	86,931
1981	113,251	77.3	22,683	15.5	10,263	7.2	146,197
1982	83,696	70.6	24,688	20.5	10,263	8.6	118,647
1983	93,745	76.8	16,699	16.1	8,607	7.1	119,051
1984	99,879	77.3	19,392	15.0	9,926	7.7	129,197
1985	72,466	72.7	19,092	19.1	8,276	8.3	99,834

*Percentage of year's total.

Source: Husbands, Winston. 1989. "Social Status and Perception of Tourism in Zambia." *Annals of Tourism Research.* 16: 240.

structure, amenities, and exposures to other cultures—that they would not have if tourism was not encouraged.

It is imperative for nations attempting to expand or operate a tourist industry to fully understand the economic benefits and costs of such endeavors. Generally, some of the most prominent factors that impact the economy are as follows:

1. The nature of the main facility and its attractiveness to tourists.

2. The volume and intensity of tourist expenditures in the destination area.

3. The level of economic development of the destination area.

4. The size of the economic base of the destination area.

5. The degree to which tourist expenditures recirculate within the destination.

6. The degree to which the destination has adjusted to the seasonability of tourist demand (Mathieson and Wall 1982).

African nations like Botswana, Lesotho, and Swaziland have attempted to develop a tourist industry, but evidence shows that little has been achieved in these countries, although the industry flourished in the 1970s and attracted many South Africans. Political and economic changes disrupted the progress.

Historically, tourism development in Africa has received little encouragement because colonial rulers did not plan for the industry to be a major income earner for the African countries. Few facilities were provided by colonial governments and little encouragement was given to host governments to invest in the industry, but African countries with great potential for tourism development should have developed the resources sooner and learned to manage the resources properly to enjoy their benefits in perpetuity.

Foreign Exchange and Employment Effects of Tourism in Africa

For the countries shown in Table 6, tourism is a major foreign exchange earner. Recognizing the importance of tourism in countries like Kenya, Uganda, Zambia, and Zaire, international financial institutions have encouraged projects in several African countries. It should also be pointed out that the threat of losing magnificent African animals to poachers has accelerated the coordinated international efforts to discourage international trade that could destroy the balance of the African ecosystem. For example, in Kenya alone, about one thousand elephants were being killed per week, but, with the efforts of foreign institutions and the Kenyan government, the poachers are being challenged, laws are being enforced, and

Table 6
Comparative Data on International Tourism in Selected Developing Countries, 1970

	Estimated Foreign Visitor Arrivals	Average Length of Stay of Foreign Visitors (Overnight)	Gross Foreign Tourism Receipts ($ million)	Average Daily Foreign Tourist Expenditures ($)	Gross Tourism Receipts Compared with Merchandise Exports ($)
East Africa					
Ethiopia	53	4.0	6	28.0	4.9
Kenya	344	8.8	52	16.8	24.0
Tanzania	63	9.0	14	24.8	5.6
Uganda	80	9.7	19	24.0	7.7
West Africa					
Ivory Coast	42	4.0	5	30.0	1.5
Senegal	40	3.5	4	25.0	2.6

Source: World Bank. 1972. *Tourism: Sector Working Paper.* Washington, D.C.: The World Bank, p. 30.

local residents are being informed about the significance of the wildlife (*Science News* 1988).

Zaire is enjoying an increase in the tourism business because of the international awareness of the importance of gorillas and elephants. Documentaries are being made about these animals; that means economic benefits for the country. Tables 7 and 8 indicate the assistance offered to some African countries so that they can continue to develop their tourism industries. It must be emphasized that banks attempt to evaluate projects in the context of the tourism sector. In other words, they conduct an assessment of the range of the country's tourism assets and their value to the economy of the country as a whole.

It is obvious from the opposing theoretical discussions that tourism development is not for all countries in Africa. Tourism development should be undertaken only by those countries that will benefit from the global growth and trends of tourism. These countries have to be self-reliant, and the development must be gradual, taking into consideration the local culture and the participation of the host citizens in all levels of management. This will mean training the local residents. Such ventures could be expen-

Table 7

Tourism Financing by the International Finance Corporation

Country/ Project	Original Amount of IFC Commitment or Approval ($ thousand)	Date of Original Commitment or Approval	Investment held by IFC as of December 31, 1971 ($ thousand)			Comments
			Equity	Loan	Total	
Kenya/Hotel						
Properties	3,204	1967/1968	561	1,550	2,111	Part-financing of 200-room hotel in capital city, some game lodges, and 100-room beach hotel
Tunisia/						
Cie.Financiere						
et Touristique	9,905	1969	1,905	6,891	8,796	Tourism development and holding company
Kenya & Uganda/						
Tourism Promotion Services, Ltd.	(K) 2,420 (U) 1,180 16.709	1971	--- 2.466	3,600 12.041	3,600 14.507	Financing of hotels and lodges comprising 950 beds and 138-vehicle touring service

Source: World Bank. 1972. *Tourism: Sector Working Paper.* Washington, D.C.: The World Bank, p. 31.

sive initially, but in the long run, they are cost-effective. Since tourism requires a systems approach to its development, management, and marketing, tourism planners in Africa must not rush into the implementation of their plans. They must employ methodologies that would make tourism development an integral part of the total economic development of their countries.

CONCLUSIONS AND INFERENCES

The establishment of multinational firms in developing countries induces the displacement of local indigenous companies. The impact is severe because a whole range of small, semiskilled, and skilled local production is slowed down and in many cases displaced. It takes a great deal of effort, energy, and local money for small businesses in African countries to be established. In many cases, extended family members

Table 8
Commitments for Tourism Projects under World Bank Loans to
Development Finance Companies

Country	Name of Company	Number of Projects	Bank Funds Committed by OFSs as of December 31, 1971 ($ thousand)
Tunisia	Societe Nationale d'Investissement	32	14,510
Morocco	Credit Immobilier et Hotelier	22	3,131
Morocco	Banque Nationale de Developement Economique	22	7,871
	TOTAL	76	30,512

Source: World Bank. 1972. *Tourism: Sector Working Paper.* Washington, D.C.: The World Bank, p. 32.

contribute money and time in order to get the entrepreneurial venture started. The establishment of multinational corporations destroys the local business ventures. The experience of Nigeria indicates that the practices of the colonial rulers created a disadvantageous situation for indigenous African business men and women. Biersteker (1978:68–69) notes:

Policies directed toward foreign investors during the colonial period have had far reaching implications for both the Nigerian economy in general and subsequent, postindependence foreign investment policies. Although they consistently opposed the acquisition of land and establishment of plantations by Europeans, the colonial authorities enacted legislation that not only tolerated but supported the growth of large expatriate trading firms in Nigeria. By imposing heavy trading licenses and stringent marketing regulations and by sending primitive expectations against resisting Africans, the colonial government eliminated indigenous competitors and opened the way for an "unimpeded take over" of the economy by expatriate firms.

African governments create the circumstances that make it difficult for indigenous firms to compete with the multinationals. Tax relief is given to multinationals, and African governments give them assurances to attract them to invest. For instance, during the 1950s British multinationals were given the freedom to repatriate profits, dividends, and capitals without any restriction from any Nigerian government—be it federal or regional (Biersteker 1978).

Since the main motivation for the multinational firm is to make a profit, very few or no indigenous African firms are given the opportunity to participate in the research and development conducted by multinationals, and as such very little development takes place in Africa. Biersteker (1978:121) gives evidence of a study conducted by the Nigerian Council for Science and Technology in 1971 indicating that of the 309 firms responding to a survey, only 13 percent conducted research and development in Nigeria. Technologically, transnational firms have had a tremendous impact on developing countries. This impact did not begin in the 1980s or 1990s; it began during the colonial era. During this period, Africans were restricted from engaging in the ownership of major technological operations such as mining ventures. The role of Africans was restricted to unskilled labor. European colonialism impeded the gradual progress that Africans had been making technologically; historically, Africans were engaged in small mining operations before the arrivals of Europeans in Africa (Rodney 1974).

Multinational investment in Africa in technological areas has not really improved or enhanced development because very little research and development (R&D) is carried out in African countries. This leads one to argue that technology transfer to Africa may not be appropriate. Multinational firms influence the sociocultural changes in many African countries as well as other developing countries of the world (Mattelart 1983). A good example for this argument is the consumption pattern of African countries. The apparel industries of many African countries have been invaded by multinational cooperations. This can be seen from the clothing pattern of many urban and rural settings of African countries. Local traders of traditional clothing have slowly been losing their market share to foreign competitors. The younger generations are more interested in foreign-made, Western-style clothes and goods. The net result is that there is a rapid cultural change brought about as a result of the multinationals' presence in Africa. Their impact can be seen in the media, in education, books, journals, magazines, and cosmetic products.

This chapter is not an attempt to argue that everything done by multinationals is bad but to point out that Africans must recognize the impact of multinationals on development strategies and must conduct benefit-cost-risk analysis in choosing which multinationals they should do business with. The trade-offs made by Africans and African countries should not jeopardize or mortgage the future of generations to come. The human and natural (renewable and nonrenewable) resources can be useful in perpetuity when they are not mismanaged.

4 WATER QUALITY MANAGEMENT PLANNING IN DEVELOPING COUNTRIES: AN INTERDISCIPLINARY APPROACH

In the 1980s the world witnessed many ecological disasters in the developing countries. These catastrophes included famine in several African countries, such as Ethiopia and the Sudan, accelerated desertification, air and water pollution, and the threat to some endangered animals in Africa. The attention of world leaders, policymakers, and planners has now turned to threats to the survival of the human race. Planners in the developing and developed countries now have to answer the question of whether the tools that have been created to address environmental problems are suitable for the developing countries.

THE CURRENT SITUATION

Attempting to understand the magnitude of the ecological problem in developing countries, one can find two views of the crisis in the developing countries' literature. One, presented in several publications by the United Nations, sees these countries as impoverished and miserable. These publications generally conclude with optimism. The second view is presented by individual scholars and researchers in studies that are generally ideological and methodological in nature. They discuss individual cities and politics and the problems associated with burgeoning cities, squatters, unemployment, poor housing conditions, public services that are poorly financed and managed, and population increase (Qadeer 1983). In the developing countries, increase in population, urbanization, transportation, and tourism have accelerated the pressures on land development. These countries must develop national comprehensive environmental plans in order to manage their natural resources. In order for the resources to be managed effectively, the different disciplines concerned with environmental management have to work in an integrated manner. The concept of carrying capacity has not been clearly defined for humans, but every resource has its limits with respect to how much use it can support before it is overused. Planners in developing countries should find the concept of carrying capacity to be a useful tool that could be incorporated into their environmental management planning (Beale 1975).

Presently, there are few studies that discuss environmental planning as part of a national or regional development plan. Many developing countries define their development plans without giving proper attention to environmental planning. The reason for such a strategy is twofold: (1) because development plans in developing countries are part of economic development and (2) because there is no interdisciplinary approach to problem solving in these countries. Thus, the point of departure for this chapter is that environmental consideration should be included in the overall planning of the developing nations since these countries depend heavily on their natural resources. Such environmental considerations should include, among other things, water quality management as an ecological concern.

In order to understand the current situation of the need for water quality management and development in the developing countries, one needs to examine the progress made by some of these nations during the World Drinking Water and Sanitation Decade. It is estimated that more than half of the people of the Third World do not have safe drinking water and that three-quarters of the population have no safe sanitation. Since polluted water and lack of sanitation are responsible for more than 80 percent of the world's diseases, there is a need for improvement of water quality management in the developing world. By 1980, the World Health Organization concluded that about 25 million people were killed by diarrhea; half of this number were children. The launching of the World Drinking Water and Sanitation Decade by the United Nations was meant to improve the quality of life of the peoples of the world by assisting in the development of better sanitation systems and water resources.

The gross national product is low for many of these countries, but high infant mortality, low life expectancy, and water-borne diseases can all be ameliorated with improvements in provisions of safe drinking water and sanitation to both the urban and rural populations.

In providing safe drinking water and good sanitation systems in developing countries, some countries set their target dates at 1990. Unfortunately many of the African countries did not meet their target supply of safe water and sanitation for both urban and rural communities. From many indications, based on the 1987 situation in these countries, the 1990 targets will not be achieved, but the encouraging news is that progress is being made. The World Bank is examining ways of encouraging the participation of the indigenous inhabitants in the planning of the water and sanitation projects.

THE FRAMEWORK

The technical portion of the planning process is concerned with identifying the priority of water quality problems of the developing nations, recognizing the constraints in dealing with the problems, and developing alternatives to achieve water quality goals. A nation's water quality management plan is the overall framework within which regional plans must be developed for specific portions of the country. Water quality management plans must contain the following elements: (1) water quality standards and goals, (2) definition of critical water quality conditions, and (3) a provision for waste load and constraints. Regional plans must be integral parts of the developing countries' water quality management plans and must be reviewed annually by the ministers of the environment as being consistent with water quality management plans.

THE INFLUENCE OF AGRICULTURE

The developing countries are faced with the problem of continued population growth. One of the answers to this problem is to increase agricultural activities, including the use of fertilizers on farms. Poor farming practices will result in the pollution of the streams and rivers. Urban runoff and erosion of agricultural lands are other sources of water pollution in developing countries.

The water quality management plan for developing countries should contain specific recommendations for the abatement of agricultural nonpoint pollution. Agencies should be set up to give technical assistance to farmers so that the latter can deal with the problem of water pollution and, more important, soil erosion. The town planning offices in the developing countries must have a coordinated effort in order to implement effective land use control (Lesaca 1974).

All lands are subject to natural degradation processes that cause sediments to be eroded and transported to other places. This process of natural pollution can be observed all over the world; it is exacerbated by humans. The particular types and amounts of urban and rural nonpoint pollutants entering surface waters are dependent upon the characteristics of the land that generates them and the mechanism by which they are transported (Water Resources Council 1973). Several methods are available for controlling nonpoint source pollution. Nonpoint source pollution in the developing countries, like anywhere else in the world, results from the use and management of large acres of land. It occurs predominantly during the rainy seasons. Experience from the United States shows that the only successful method of controlling this type of pollution is to prevent its occurrence. This strategy depends on several conditions, such as soil, topography, drainage, climate, and so forth, of the country (Troeh and Thompson 1978).

In dealing with cropland runoff, the strategy calls for the following method: (1) crop rotation, in which different crops are grown in sequential pattern on the same field; (2) conservation tillage system, in which a number of minimum tillage practices are used to reduce erosion potential; (3) grassed outlet system, which can be used for preventing nonpoint source pollution through construction of outlets established with erosion restraint vegetation; (4) and the terrace system, another method that can be used to prevent nonpoint pollution (Browning and Parish 1947).

As mentioned earlier, the geometric increase in the population of the developing countries will force their governments to adopt policies that focus attention on family planning, agricultural research, and crop production. Some assistance will be given to farmers in the form of fertilizers to increase food production (Seaborg 1969). In order to enhance the protection of the water quality supply in developing countries, water quality plans should include control of fertilizers. To deal with this problem, (1) there should be an education of farmers on the proper application of fertilizers, involving not only the use of soil tests to avoid excessive application but also care in the timing of application, and (2) crop rotation of leguminous plants should be used to enhance crop production.

SEWAGE TREATMENT

In some developing countries, raw sewage is deposited directly into the rivers and streams. This action constitutes a health hazard to the public at large because rivers and streams serve as sources of drinking water and fish.

Septic systems are common in both urban and rural areas of many developing countries. The water quality management plan should include control of septic systems, which should be used where the soil is found to be suitable by geologists, hydrologists, and health officials. Sewage treatment plants are expensive, but the health benefits that can be derived by having them far outweigh the cost of installing such plants. It must also be stressed that the cost-effectiveness of the plants exceeds that of any other method currently used in these countries. In attempting to compare costs and benefits of water pollution abatement, policymakers are faced with several complications. One is that estimates of benefits are not absolute. Another is that there are benefits other than those relating to health. A third complication is that abstract cost estimates are incomplete because they ignore impacts on productivity and economic growth. Systematic planning is necessary for every waste water disposal scheme. The nature of such a program will determine the extent and direction of the planning effort. The extension or improvement of an established system would entail a consideration of past performance and a review of a large amount of available physical data. In developing countries, records are not properly kept, hence the availability of data is a major problem. Modern water quality requirements demand the planning of collection and disposal systems in rural areas where old private septic systems have failed.

CITIZEN PARTICIPATION

Assessing benefits implies a standard of measurement. Benefits imply satisfaction, which in turn implies preferences and expectations. Decisions on water quality management planning are not made by individuals but by governments that express the collective judgments of some of their constituents. In the Western countries, water quality management is unique because local citizens and officials interact during the planning process. This is not the case in many developing countries. The success of water quality management planning in developing countries depends on education of the general public on critical water quality issues and the subsequent contribution of the public to the planning process of water quality management. The average citizen in developing countries may not have detailed expertise in the area of water quality management but would like to be consulted. The challenge then is for the governments to increase the public's knowledge of environmental issues and in so doing to improve environmental decision-making processes.

CONCLUSIONS AND RECOMMENDATIONS

With the proliferation of population and technology, humankind has the capacity to destroy itself through the disruption of natural ecosystems. This chapter has amplified some of the current concerns of the planners and policymakers in the developing countries in regard to environmental problems they face, with particular emphasis on how development and human activities can cause the pollution of the water in these countries. Water pollution can be reduced by controlling activities that result in the deterioration of the environment. The manner of the disposal of sewage should be given serious consideration. Regional water management agencies should be set up to enhance the coordination of a national effort. Such agencies will assist in the enforcement of water quality control. Basic human needs such as water and food depend upon the quality of natural resources planning and management strategies.

5 PROBLEMS OF AGRICULTURAL PRODUCTION: SOIL CONDITIONS

The two major environmental determinants of agricultural production are soil conditions and climate. There is an urgent need for the farmers of developing nations to take into consideration these environmental factors when planning for food production. Since there are variations in the soil conditions and climate from place to place, regions within the same tropical climate of Africa can have different soil conditions.

Soil experts argue that two ways of studying the potential productivity of soils (soil-crop relationship) are (1) to have a sound knowledge of crops with respect to particular environmental conditions (in this case, soil), and (2) to have a knowledge of plant diseases. Nonetheless, the knowledge of how soil properties influence the growing conditions of crops is pertinent to the study of the problem of agricultural production in Africa.

CLASSES OF AFRICAN SOILS

Generally, there are sandy, silt, and clay soils in Africa. In some places, loam soil (a mixture of sand, silt, and clay) is found. African soils are formed through the interaction of parent rock, topography, vegetation, and organic matter. Although soil classification is muddled by many disagreements, the FAO (1973) has published a comprehensive map that categorizes the major soils of the world. Figure 11 shows the major soils of Africa. It must be pointed out that this is a classification of soil mapping units and not a systematic classification. Their descriptions are as follows: (1) The entisols are found predominantly in the central half of the continent and in the desert areas of the north. The soils of recent alluvium are commonly of this type and have little or no profile development. (2) The

Figure 11
Major Soils of Africa

A   ALFISOLS
D   ARIDISOLS
E   ENTISOLS
I   INCEPTISOLS
O   OXISOLS
U   ULTISOLS
V   VERTISOLS
X   SOILS IN AREAS
     WITH MOUNTAINS

Source: U.S. Soil Conservation Service. 1972. *Soil Map of the World*. Washington, D.C.: The Soil Geography Unit of USSCS, 43.

vertisols, found predominantly in East Africa, are the heavy, dark clay soils that develop wide cracks during the dry season. In the rainy season, the cracks are filled with small soil aggregates that result in the formation of microreliefs called gilgai. The vertisols are also characterized by their high water retention; unfortunately, only a small amount of water is available for plant utilization and they succumb easily to erosion. (3) The aridisols are found in the arid regions and are usually dry but become saline through contact with water (seepage). (4) The inceptisols are young soils with limited profile development. (5) The histosols are found in isolated places in Africa. They are generally made up of organic substances and are sometimes referred to as "peat soils." They can also be found in flat high elevations (Buringh 1979). (6) Mollisols, spondosols, alfisols, ultisols, and oxisols are the other types of soils found in Africa. Generally, these soils are limited in fertility.

Scholarly and professional research on Africa's agricultural failure has attempted to establish the causes of and potential solutions to the alarming problems that agriculture is facing in a continent among the richest in natural resources. It is only appropriate that an attempt be made to investigate whether agricultural failure is predominant among certain soil types.

The moisture and temperature regimes of an area's soils are important in understanding the agricultural productivity of the area. Figure 12 shows the moisture and temperature regimes of Africa. The aridic conditions are numbered 1 to 8. These represent the situation when the soils are dry for an extensive part of the year. Such soils are generally found within the desertlike parts of Africa. Buringh (1979) estimates that in the tropics the aridic regimes may not be dry for about sixty days, while in the subtropics of Africa the aridic regimes are not dry for ninety consecutive days. In the aquic moisture regime, it has been shown that groundwater reaches down into the subsoil. This regime can be found in western and eastern Africa, along the Niger, Nile, and Congo rivers. In the udic regime, the soils are generally moist for more than 270 days of the year. The ustic regime, which is represented by numbers 14–17 in Figure 12, is made up of soils that are rich in moisture for more than 180 days of the year. The xeric regime, found in the extreme northern and southern coasts of Africa, enjoys the mediterranean climate; thus the soil is moist in the cool winter and dry during the growing summer season. The more wet days a regime has, the better is its agricultural productivity.

The temperature regimes of soils play important roles in agricultural productivity. Extremely cold or hot temperatures are destructive to crops. In most of Africa, it is the extreme heat, coupled with drought, that inhibits crop production.

There are other soil properties that are pertinent to the agricultural potentiality of soils. Among these are (1) rooting depth and volume, the depth to which the roots of crops and other plants can penetrate the soil and the actual volume in which the roots are observed (not soil volume); (2) stratification; (3) content of organic matter; (4) base saturation; (5) homogenization; and (6) mineral composition. The description of some of these properties is beyond the scope of this research. Suffice it to mention

Figure 12
Soil Moisture and Temperature Regimes in Africa

1. ARIDIC, THERMIC
2. ARIDIC, ISOTHERMIC
3. ARIDIC, HYPERTHERMIC
4. ARIDIC, ISOHYPERTHERMIC
5. ARIDIC, MESIC AND FRIGID
6. ARIDIC TO USTIC, THERMIC
7. ARIDIC TO USTIC, HYPERTHERMIC
8. ARIDIC TO USTIC, ISOHYPERTHERMIC
9. AQUIC, THERMIC
10. AQUIC, ISOHYPERTHERMIC
11. UDIC, ISOHYPERTHERMIC
12. UDIC TO USTIC, THERMIC
13. UDIC TO USTIC, ISOHYPERTHERMIC
14. USTIC, THERMIC
15. USTIC, ISOTHERMIC
16. USTIC, HYPERTHERMIC
17. USTIC, ISOHYPERTHERMIC
18. XERIC, THERMIC

Source: Buringh, P. 1979. *Introduction to the Study of Soils in Tropical and Subtropical Regions.* Wageningen, The Netherlands: Center for Agricultural and Publishing Documentation, p. 3.

that these characteristics are important to the agricultural productivity of the soils. For example, the organic matter decomposition forms the upper layer of the soil, humus, which is very important for the crops. Crops need a variety of mineral nutrients for their proper development. Soils deficient in mineral nutrients are not good for agriculture.

African soils, like the soils of other tropical continents, have the potential for crop production. The poor manipulation of the soils and forests through the intensification of traditional agricultural systems and the introduction of mechanized agriculture pose a great threat to the natural resources. Figure 13 depicts the potential of the land. As can be seen, many of the areas that are located in the southern boundaries of the Sahara Desert and on the northern and eastern edges of the Kalahari Desert have some agricultural potential. The question that has to be answered now is how the African countries can manage their resources adequately in order to produce sufficient food for their growing population. Part of the answer will be answered by tackling the problem of soil erosion.

SOIL EROSION

Due to shifting agricultural systems, African soils face the danger of erosion. The process of soil erosion occurs naturally and has great geological importance. The productive valleys, plains, and highlands of Africa owe their richness to the process of erosion. The nourishment for fish populations in African rivers, streams, and lagoons is due to erosion. Hence it must be emphasized that natural erosion has positive impacts on the ecological systems of Africa, but the encroaching human population and the demand for fuel wood coupled with shifting cultivation are exacerbating erosion problems. Unfortunately, this condition prevails in most of the savanna and forest regions of Africa. Researchers claim that the Sahara was once teeming with life (plant and animal). It was occupied by people who abused the natural resources and deforestation was followed by desertification. Erosion played a significant role in the formation of the Sahara (James 1987a; Myers 1984).

The Process of Soil Formation

The rate of soil formation differs from one climatic region to another. As mentioned earlier, soil formation depends on four principal factors: parent rock, topography, climate, vegetation, and fauna found in the area. In the tropical rain forest of Africa, the rate of soil formation is faster than that of a cultivated land in the savanna. Heller (1962) suggests that it will take between 100 to 300 years to form a soil cover of a foot thick naturally. Soil formation in all the African biomes is a dynamic process. It entails the combination of organic and inorganic substances. Upon achieving equilibrium, a superficial stability is observed, but, in reality, the dynamic process is continuous. Soil is the foundation upon which the other natural resources of the ecosystem depend. The complexity of the soil demands that care should be taken in the cultivation of the land. The misuse of the vegetation can set up a chain reaction that destroys the fertility of the soil (U.S. Agency for International Development 1985).

Figure 13
Agricultural Potential of African Land

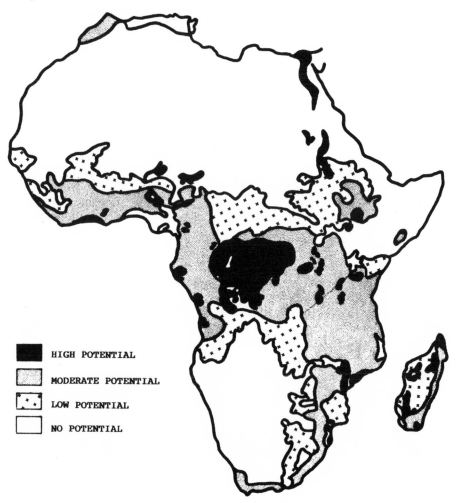

HIGH POTENTIAL

MODERATE POTENTIAL

LOW POTENTIAL

NO POTENTIAL

The Process of Soil Erosion

Misuse of land is almost always to blame for accelerated erosion that occurs in Africa. The manipulation of the natural vegetation through cultivation or overgrazing by cattle, sheep, or goats leads to the exposure of the topsoil to direct rainfall and sunlight. Such a situation leads to leaching and the desiccation of the fertile topsoil. Excessive cutting of trees and burning of forests have negative impacts on the soil (U.S. Office of Technology Assessment 1983). The erosion of soils that have been denuded of vegetation operates in a number of ways. Strong winds blow away the fertile soil layers, leaving infertile layers that are not helpful to the growth of crops. This type of erosion prevails during the summer. In the rainy seasons, topsoils are washed away from the slopes. A soil regions map (Figure 14) is used to describe the fertility of the soil in West Africa. In region 1 (along the coast), the soil is poor for many crops because of its deficiency in bases. In region 2, heavy rainfall leads to desalination, and the soils have drainage problems, making the harvesting of rice difficult. In region 3, which is mainly freshwater coastal swamps, many crops such as rice are grown. The soils of region 4 are formed from old consolidated rocks. They are deficient in phosphorus but are very good for the cultivation of cessan. This region is extensive in Liberia and Sierra Leone. In region 5, the soils are formed from unconsolidated younger sands and is most suitable for oil palm. Region 6 falls within the forest and savanna where sorghum (*Sorghum bicolor*), pearl millet (*Pennisestum americanum*), voandzeia (*Voandzeia subterranea*), rice (*Oryza glaberrima*), cotton (*Gossypium herbaceum*), fonio (*Digitaria exilis*), roselle (*Hibiscus sabdariffa*), watermelon (*Citrulus lanatus*), karite (*Butyrospermum paradoxum*), parkia (*Parkia species*), sesame (*Sesamamum indicum*) (if African) are grown (Harlan, DeWet, and Stember 1976). Region 7 contains soils formed from unconsolidated younger sands. They have great depths, which prove to be conducive for the cultivation of oil palm. Region 8 contains soils formed from young continental deposits. Continuous cultivation can be practiced on this soil and it can support high populations. Vertisols are found in this region. In region 9, located predominantly along the Volta River, many of the soils found here are formed from unweatherable substances. Rice crop is cultivated here because of the abundant water. Region 10 can be found in the lower Volta plains. It comprises mainly vertisols and gray earth (clay-pan planosols and sodium vertisols).

In West Africa, there is a soil region that is made up of gray to black plastic clays, predominantly vertisols. This is shown as region 11 in Figure 14. The soils of this region (Chad Basin) have been found to be rich in bases, which make them suitable for cultivating rice, sugar cane, vegetables, and cotton. However, this area is prone to flood; thus flood regulation, drainage, and irrigation are pertinent to the successful cropping of the land adjacent to the lake (FAO 1978). Generally, it should be pointed out that, in southern and central parts of Africa where the rainfall is high and water is nearly percolating through the soil, the fine particles of the topsoil are washed into the subsoil. This is why the subsoil is richer in mineral nutrients than the surface soil. In spite of the fact that tropical African soils are deficient in calcium and phosphates (in comparison with the soils of temperate climates), they have productive potentials.

It is incorrect to assume that tropical African soils are mediocre or poor.

Figure 14
Soil Regions Map of West Africa

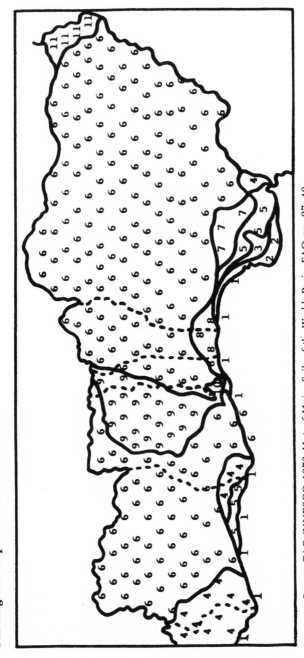

Source: FAO/UNESCO 1973 *Map of Major Soils of the World.* Paris: FAO pp. 27–40.

1. *Soils deficient in bases*
2. *Soils with desalination and drainage problems*
3. *Soils of fresh water coastal swamps*
4. *Soils of old consolidated rocks*
5. *Soils of unconsolidated younger rocks*

6. *Soils of the forest and savanna*
7. *Soils conducive for oil palm*
8. *Soils can support continuous cultivation*
9. *Soils formed from unweatherable substances*
10. *Mainly vertisols*
11. *Soils of black plastic clays*

The moist rain-forest region proves that there can be luxuriant growth in Africa if natural resources are not abused. Soil is one of the most important natural resources of Africa. Its proper use and conservation is crucial to the maintenance of all forms of life, including the human population. As mentioned previously, the population increase is making traditional agricultural systems the culprits in the destruction of African natural resources. With increasing demand for agricultural land and other forms of land use, soil erosion problems are increasing in Africa. The use of chemical fertilizer is increasing and will continue to increase in the next two decades if Africans are to feed themselves. Along with this increase is the problem of soil erosion. Deforestation due to the cutting and burning of trees denies the soil the protection it receives from the leaves of trees and exposes the topsoil to the direct rays of the sun. In the forest region, such deforestation exposes the soil to heavy rainfall, which leads to leaching. The laterite left is infertile for cultivation. In the savanna region, trees are fewer and cutting and burning destroys existing ecosystems. The cutting and burning in shifting cultivation exposes the soil to sheet erosion during the rainy season. In the savanna of West Africa, sheet erosion occurs over a large area of land. The topsoil is washed away because the soil surface does not absorb the rainwater readily (FAO 1978). This type of erosion has led to reduction in soil profiles of some land areas in Africa. It must, however, be pointed out again that this problem persists in agricultural areas and in areas experiencing tremendous population pressures.

It is estimated in the FAO/Unesco (1973) soils map of the world that 44 percent of Africa experiences drought and 18 percent of the continent is made up of soils that are deficient in mineral nutrients necessary for the cultivation of crops. African soils have the unique characteristic of being thin; it is estimated that 13 percent of the continent has soils that are shallow in depth, thus making it difficult for crops and trees to anchor themselves properly. Nine percent of African land contains excess water during the rainy season, thus making it almost impossible to grow crops, especially along the deltas of the Niger and the Volta. The precarious situation of sheet and gully erosions can be avoided if the forests are properly used and managed. Serious erosion occurs along the slopes of hills and mountains of Africa.

Severe problems with the soil and climate of many African countries restrict large populations to small areas of arable land, a situation that hinders food production efforts and that has prompted governments such as Gambia to initiate national soil surveys. Efforts to establish a conservation program in a developing country are bound to be far more complicated than merely applying Western technology to combat the deteriorating situation of natural resources. The culture, tradition, religion, and economy of the African countries must be taken into consideration when planning for soil conservation.

In Africa, gullies are generally found in areas with steep slopes. The runoff digs waterways and gradually cuts deep gullies, which increase the erosive processes. Data from Zimbabwe show that where bare soil is exposed to the rain, the annual soil loss varies from 25 to 225 tons a year from each acre on slopes of 3 percent to 6.5 percent. Under the same conditions, soil loss from a grass-covered area does not exceed half a ton per acre (Golley 1975).

During the past century, water and wind erosion have removed an estimated 5 billion acres of soil in various parts of the world. That is the equivalent of over a quarter of the erosion caused by the earth's farmlands, grazed pastures, unprotected forest soils, strip mines, roads, road banks, and all types of bulldozed areas. In fact, agricultural development increases land erosion rates up to ten times over what they are for natural cover, while construction may increase the rate a hundredfold. Sediments carried by erosion resulting from human activity represent the greatest volume of wastes entering surface waters.

Plant cover eliminates the erosive effects of raindrops hitting the bare ground and greatly reduces runoff and water loss (Hopkins 1973). In well-balanced ecosystems, where forest and other kinds of vegetation protect mountain slopes and habitats beneath the trees, catastrophic erosion does not occur, and the hydrography of the country contributes to the fertility of the soil. People should take advantage of such optimal situations, which provide the basis for sustained yields of whatever the land produces.

The conservation of soil resources is among the most important tasks confronting governments all over the world. On all continents except Antarctica, erosion is a major hazard to the future of humankind, but few countries seem to be aware of how serious the situation is. The African countries that are aware of the seriousness of this problem have not addressed it adequately. While tragic, this is perhaps not so remarkable, because the catastrophic situations are the results of continuous misuse of land for thousands of years. The cause is human beings alone. The climate cannot be blamed for the mismanagement of the earth's resources.

In Africa, the desert is now spreading over larger and larger areas of the Mediterranean region. Two or three thousand years ago, many areas of North Africa were fertile lands supporting flourishing civilizations, mighty kingdoms, and large populations. Today, the same areas are pure deserts that cannot support human habitation (James 1987b).

There are many indications that the spread of the North African deserts is primarily due to cutting of trees and overgrazing by cattle and goats. During Phoenician, Roman, French, and Italian civilization in North Africa, when the governments were stable and progressive, vegetation slowly reconquered the desert. But every time the Arabs returned to power nomadic tribes and their livestock invaded the fertile areas, which soon collapsed due to misuse, and deserts again took over. The same phenomenon is to be seen in the southern Sahara at the edge of the savannas. Likewise, in many parts of East Africa, West Africa, South Africa, and the Malagasy Republic, the deserts are spreading in previously fertile country at alarming rates. As soon as overgrazing by cattle, goats and sheep occurs, or farmers practice unwise agricultural methods, protective savannas with comparatively rich vegetation and wildlife rapidly disappear and give way to deserts. Dunes that have been kept in place by the vegetation for centuries revert to moving sand waves, killing everything in their path. River sources dry up, and so does the land along the dry river beds. The rains, no longer stored by the vegetation, sink deep down into the earth or run off, carrying fertile soils down to the sea (Golley 1975).

Studies of the prime causes of erosion damage in Africa and other parts of the world show that it has been preceded by overgrazing and overtrampling by livestock and unwise methods of cultivation—the types of land use that tend to remove and destroy the vegetation cover. The results are that the whole ecosystem has been disrupted.

One of the worst consequences of erosion is its influence on the local climate and hydrography. Lowering water tables often follow in its steps: Water is no longer stored in upper soil layers, and it becomes inaccessible to plants and animals. Dry seasons, which previously were a normal occurrence, tend to develop into drought catastrophes, embracing a much wider region than the eroded area. The African continent cannot afford the continuous devastating consequences of drought. One-fifth of the camels in the eastern Sahara have perished because of drought in the early 1980s (James 1987b).

SOME TECHNIQUES FOR CONSERVING SOIL

Erosion involves detachment and transportation of soil particles. Erosion control practices can be aimed at reducing either detachment or transportation, or both. For example, a vegetative cover or a mulch on the soil surface prevents detachment because it prevents raindrops from striking the soil surface. Rough contour plowing may permit detachment but prevents transportation because water is held in depressions until it infiltrates the soil (Curry-Lindahl 1972).

The most appropriate type of control measure depends on the type and severity of erosion hazards and the nature of the soil. In general, the particles in sandy soils are easily detached but are difficult to transport. Erosion control practices that limit runoff to slow velocity are highly effective for conserving sandy soils. The particles in soils high in clay are usually difficult to detach, but easy to transport. It is more practical to limit detachment of particles from clay soils than to prevent detached particles from being transported.

Aggregate stability is a major variable that is well correlated with soil erodibility. Soils containing significant amounts of clay form aggregates with varying degrees of stability. Unstable aggregates break apart under the impact of raindrops. Some silt and clay particles broken from aggregates are carried away in runoff water; other particles are carried into soil pores and tend to lodge there. The crust thus formed has a low permeability and results in a greatly increased runoff and erosion. Stable aggregates resist raindrop impact for a much longer time and maintain the soil in a more permeable condition.

Most soil aggregates have some cohesion from one aggregate to another, which helps soil resist erosion. Some aggregates, however, have strong internal cohesion, but little or no external cohesion to other aggregates. Soils dominated by such aggregates behave like sandy soils as far as erosion is concerned, even if they have high clay content.

There are two major methods of erosion control: vegetative and mechanical methods. Vegetative methods can be highly effective at controlling erosion. Natural prairie and forest vegetation normally limit erosion to less than half a ton of soil loss per acre per year. Very few cropped fields have such low soil losses, even if they are protected by intensive erosion control practices (Knuti, Korpi, and Hide 1970). An important consideration is an appropriate vegetation cover for the land. In urban and suburban areas, along highways, and so on, this usually means selection of the types of grass, flowers, shrubs, and trees to be grown. A second consideration in growing crops is the plant population or number of plants per acre. Appropriate varieties and high fertility may make it possible to grow more plants per acre and thus reduce the open space between plants. Row crops may be grown with narrower row spacing to permit them to protect more of the soil from erosion. There are several methods of controlling erosion. Descriptions of vegetative methods of controlling erosion follow.

Cover Crops

The principal crops in a rotation may leave the soil unprotected at times. A cover crop must be fast-growing so that it can be established after the harvest but before the rainy season. It must be hardy enough to tolerate the harsh weather of the area where it is grown.

The cover crop method is particularly important in Africa because it has proved to be successful in another tropical area—Malaysia. Ngin Kwi and associates (1980:30) contend that cover crops furnish protection to the soil in the following ways:

1. They protect the soil surface against the disruptive action of falling raindrops.
2. They offer resistance to moving water and slow down its rate of runoff.
3. The plant roots help to hold the soil in place.
4. The plant roots and crop residues help to improve soil structure, making it more porous and better able to absorb rainfall.

Leguminous plants have been found to be particularly good for tropical weather because of their nitrogen fixing capability. Thus, they enrich the soil in nitrogen. Upon decomposition, leguminous plants become organic matter for the formation of the topsoil, making a good foundation for the roots of crops and plants.

Companion Crops

Occasionally, two crops are grown at the same time but harvested separately. Intercropping has been shown to be successful in controlling erosion in Africa. Research conducted in Kenya showed that maize grown alongside cotton produces good results. Several other combinations of crops also provided useful results. Among those combinations, according to Wenner (1980:40), are "(1) maize and cassava, or sweet potatoes, cotton, groundnuts, simsim, pigeon peas, grams, or sun flower, (2) pigeon peas and beans or millet, (3) cotton and millet or grams or coriander, (4) bana grass and legumes." Runoff can be prevented or decreased by growing crops with fertilizer. Properly managed companion crops have a very favorable effect on erosion control. The fast-growing crop provides a thick cover later.

Strip-Cropping

A strip of close-growing vegetation placed perpendicular to the flow of the water or wind can provide protection to the adjacent strip or row of crops or of fallow land. Often a crop rotation is practiced by alternating the crops grown on the various strips. Several different applications of this practice are known as contour strip-cropping, border strip-cropping, buffer strip-cropping, field strip-cropping, and wind strip-cropping. Strip-cropping can be practiced in parts of Africa where pastures and croplands are approximately equal in size.

Windbreaks

Probably the best protection against wind erosion is a permanent vegetation cover on all land. But since the cover cannot be permanent on croplands, some kind of protection is needed for areas that must be bare during times when strong winds occur. Wind strip-cropping is a means of protecting narrow strips of bare land; windbreaks could be used to protect wider strips.

Grass Waterways

A concentrated flow of water in swales is often unavoidable. Such areas are likely places for gullies to form, especially if cultivated crops are grown in the swales. Grass waterways are used where the risk of channel erosion would be excessive if the area were cultivated. The need for a grass waterway should be recognized and acted upon early because it is much easier to prevent a gully from forming than it is to repair the land later. The easiest way to establish a grass waterway is simply to leave that portion of field unplowed when other crops follow hay or pasture.

Protecting Grazing Lands from Erosion

Extensive grazing lands are located in arid regions; small parcels are distributed almost everywhere. New vegetation is difficult to establish on much of this land because of dry weather, stony soils, steep slopes, and the like, so maintaining the vegetation already on the land is very important. Erosion control, therefore, consists of managing the livestock (Troeh and Thompson 1978).

Grazing lands produce a maximum amount of usable forage, if they are grazed moderately. Overgrazing weakens the plants and slows down growth; it also reduces the vegetative cover and increases the amount of erosion. A good rule for ranchers using semiarid rangeland is to "take half and leave half" of the year's growth. Additional care is needed to obtain uniform grazing over the entire area. Fences, water, and salt must be placed in appropriate locales to cause the livestock to cover the entire area (Moldenhauer and Amemiya 1969).

Mechanical Methods of Erosion Control

Vegetative methods can usually control erosion if they are applied soon enough, but areas that have already been seriously eroded may need mechanical methods of repair. A mechanical method may also be preferred over vegetative methods because of flexibility of land use. Vegetative methods automatically specify that certain areas must have certain vegetation. A mechanical method may permit growing a more profitable crop in these areas. Frequently, of course, vegetative and mechanical methods of conserving soil are combined to obtain maximum effectiveness. Contour strip-cropping is a good example that is partly vegetative and partly mechanical.

Contour Tillage

Row-crop farmers have traditionally taken pride in the straightness of their rows. The problem with long straight rows is that most of them come to a hill sooner or later. Cultivating makes the areas between the rows into a sloping channel lined with loose soil. Hill erosion is a very common result. Contour tillage is one of the simplest and least expensive soil conserving practices known. In fact, working around a hill rather than up and down it usually provides a saving in the form of reduced fuel consumption. Contouring may also reduce the time requirement for tillage, but this saving only occurs where the slopes are relatively smooth and uniform. Contouring is less likely to be used on rolling topography because this combination produces many point rows, crooked rows, and an increased time requirement.

Contour tillage forms small ridges across the slope. Water is stored behind the ridges and, therefore, more water infiltrates and less runs off. Contouring eliminates or greatly reduces erosion from storms heavy enough to overflow most of the ridges formed by cultivation. Contouring is most effective on gentle slopes (2 to 7 percent) of moderate length. It is less beneficial on flatter slopes than it is on gentle slopes. Tillage can be used to control wind. Both timing and type of tillage have strong influences on wind erosion. Anything that reduces wind velocity at the soil surface will reduce wind erosion. A good cover vegetation or crop residue provides excellent protection. The duration of periods without such protection depends greatly on the timing of cultivation.

Crop Residue Utilization

Most crops leave some residues behind that can be helpful in reducing soil erosion. The residues are present at the very time when protection is lacking—during the season when no crop is growing. The benefit derived from these residues depends greatly on the tillage practices. Their value for erosion control is nullified if they are plowed under long before the next crop is planted. Plowing or disking in residue so that it remains partly above the soil gives much more protection than plowing it under. The part of residues remaining above the soil gives protection from raindrop impact and reduces runoff velocities and wind velocities at the soil surface.

Mulching

Crop residues spread on soil to protect it from erosion and help it absorb water or control weeds are called mulches. Mulching is as useful on roadbanks and other construction sites as it is on fields and gardens. Construction site erosion often exceeds 100 tons per year. This method has been very effective in preventing soil erosion in many parts of the world. In parts of Kenya where banana leaves are used, the decaying leaves slow down water flows and increase the infiltration rates of the water. The mulch enhances the capability of microrganisms (insects and worms) to make their home in the soil, thus facilitating the permeability of the soil.

Terracing

Most people first think of terracing when they think of conserving soil. Terracing is usually the most effective and the most expensive method available for general field use. Many terraces are as old as the Romans in Europe and the Incas in South America. These and other ancient peoples made many hillsides look like wide giant staircases. Many of these terraces, known as bench terraces, completely eliminate the effect of slope by means of vertical stone walls. The exposed soil has a level surface and erodes no more than level bottom land erodes. Several different types of terraces have been developed in recent years.

Another method of soil erosion prevention practiced in Africa is ridging, whereby ridges are constructed by primitive methods (hand and oxen). In recent times, ridges are also constructed through the use of tractors. Ridges made with imperfect grading have the potential of causing erosion problems. Experience from some East African countries and Nigeria indicate that problems of erosion may actually be associated with bad construction of ridges. Wash stops are also used to curb erosion. There are four types of vegetation wash stops: trash limes, grass strips, fisal hedges, and bush hedges.

CONCLUSION

In conclusion, the ultimate goal of soil restoration and conservation is to put the biological processes of soil formation and soil life cycles back to work as they functioned before the vegetation was destroyed. This is a long-term task. It may well take five hundred to a thousand years or more to restore forests that once grew on mountain slopes. These forests, as well as lowland forests and grasslands, over the course of millenia had themselves created the soil humus on which they based their existence. And before the trees colonized the land, other types of vegetation, also during thousands of years, had prepared the ground for successive plant communities to evolve, building up to and producing a maximum conversion rate or energy flow in which the soil was an imperative force. Then, humanity destroyed the whole climax structure—a habitat with relatively stabilized environmental conditions—ruining not only the landscape, but also its own economy. This is what has happened and is happening increasingly over vast areas of Africa.

In many countries, particularly in the tropics and subtropics, destructive land use and increase of land-destroying livestock, as well as human population growth, hamper the effects of antierosion measures to such a degree that soil erosion accelerates despite the combat against it. The prospects of the fight for survival in such areas are not bright.

In the past, African indigenous agriculture had conservative characteristics because there was no pressure on the natural resources from the population. In the 1970s and 1980s, these characteristics have disappeared. It is not true that all traditional agricultural practices, by themselves, are wasteful, destructive, and exploitive of the natural resources of Africa.

Nonetheless, a few management strategies are suggested here in order to conserve the soil: (1) Cultivation of the savanna and forest lands should be done in small patches. (2) Such cultivations must be limited to short periods of time so that the soil can have the opportunity to regenerate its fertility. (3) The governments of developing African nations must prohibit the cutting down of large forest and savanna trees. (4) Plants with adventitious root should be grown in large quantities wherever the soil shows strong potential for erosion. The roots of such plants should be left in the ground after harvest so as to stop soil erosion during the rainy season. (5) The African fragile ecosystems must be permanently managed so that the resources can be used in perpetuity. (6) Farmers should be aware that different crops have different effects on erosion because of farm practices involved in their cultivation. The nature of the crops and the inherent properties of the soil and the African terrain must be studied on a continuous basis. Thus, the concept of proper land use must play a vital role in the conservation of the African soil. Land capability classes should be designed, on a country by country basis, to guide farmers and developers so that erosion can be prevented. Malaysia, an Asian country, has had great success with the land capability classes scheme. Finally, it must be emphasized that although African soils vary in composition, type, and properties, their response to agricultural practice seems to indicate that proper management is needed in order to sustain their fertility for crop production.

6 THE NEED FOR PROPER RESOURCE MANAGEMENT IN AFRICA

All across the continent of Africa, adequate steps must be taken to ensure that the natural resources of this great continent are not lost. Much that is yet to be discovered in the tropical rain forest would benefit the human race—not just in Africa, but all over the world. The attention of African governments, international agencies, and foreign governments is gradually moving in the direction of reversing the ecological decline in Africa, which has put human lives, wildlife, and the different ecosystems in Africa in great jeopardy. Thus, the most appropriate point of departure for this chapter is the politics of agricultural development.

POLITICAL REALITY

Many African nations have not succeeded in building strong agricultural bases because of political instability, inappropriate government policies, and misdirected priorities. Some writers, such as Dadson (1983), have argued that there are six past mistakes that must be addressed adequately if progress is to be achieved in food production in Africa: (1) The attempt to bypass traditional farmers (small-scale village farmers) in favor of large-scale production, such as state farms, settlement farms, community farms, and cooperative farms, has proven to be problematic in many African nations. Such actions are often unsuccessful because traditional farmers play an important role in the success of agriculture in Africa. Their tremendous experience with the land could be beneficial if proper incentives, in terms of appropriate technology, education, and some support, were provided. (2) Rural communities have been politically and economically neglected by the governments. In order to achieve farming success, rural communities should be included in political and economic planning. (3) In some countries, heavy machine technology and capital-intensive agriculture have been introduced. In many of these cases, such as in the highlands of Sierra Leone, mechanized agricultural practice has not increased the crop yield and has resulted in erosion problems. (4) Coercing the farmers into selling their produce at very low prices has proven to be a disincentive for crop production. (5) Poor marketing efficiency, caused by government intervention, limited capital, and inaccessibility to rural areas, has debilitating effects on agricultural production. (6) Political stability, which is necessary for economic policies to be tested and put into practice, is absent in many African nations. Every new regime discards the agendas, policies, and programs of former regimes and begins afresh. Such action leaves the farmers confused and old projects incomplete; thus, a stagnation or decline in agricultural production results.

There are many solutions to the problems mentioned so far, but the most obvious ones follow: (1) The roads and the infrastructures in these countries must be improved. (2) In order to improve the agricultural conditions, research must be conducted to maximize the productive capability of the soils. Bridges, canals, and irrigation must be provided in the rural communities to improve the quality of life of the peasant farmers. (3) Local production of fertilizers, using local raw materials, should be encouraged, and proper distribution of the fertilizers must be undertaken. Centers should be set up to assist farmers in several problem areas, such as distribution of food products, obtaining loans, and organizing the farmers into cooperatives. Such cooperatives can facilitate the sale of farm products; thus the farmers can devote more of their time to farming.

Those who have been following the global desertification process know that every year a substantial part of the earth's land (about the size of Uganda) is lost to the process of desertification. Such a piece of land becomes economically useless. The trees disappear, the soil loses its fertility, and more grazing land is lost because of past mismanagement and misuses of the natural resources. The Sahel region of Africa (Figure 15) is undergoing a tremendous change of its ecosystem.

Although over $9 billion has been put into projects in the Sahel region by several international organizations, the countries of that region, and foreign governments since the drought of early 1970s, the destruction of the savannas in this region continues on a large scale. Many researchers contend that desertification is primarily a human problem and that it could be stopped. It is a phenomenon caused by misuse, such as overgrazing, irrational cultivation, logging or wood cutting, deforestation, uprooting of plants for fuel purposes, lowering of the water table, and the

Figure 15
The Sahel Region of Africa

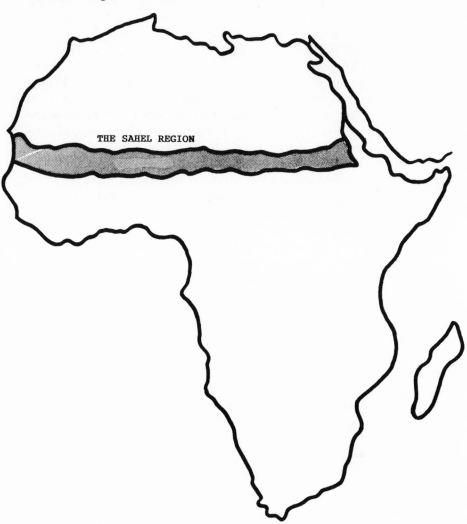

THE SAHEL REGION

slashing and burning of forests and savannas for agricultural purposes. The Sahel has a problem of high population growth rate, and on its southern fringes there is the nomadic practice of raising cattle for export to the coastal areas. The exponential increases in population and food shortages have forced small-scale farmers to cultivate marginal lands in the Sahel region of Africa. The grazing of the savanna land that otherwise would have been fallow is a common practice by the nomads in present-day Africa.

CULTURAL AND SOCIAL IMPLICATIONS

Africa is undergoing the process of modernity, which poses a problem for the nomadic lifestyle. With the influx of Western culture, technology, and education, Africa is undergoing a continuous change in ways of farming, animal husbandry, transportation, and managing its natural resources. The changes occurring in Africa will force the nomadic pastoralists to give up their present way of life, the movement from place to place in search of grazing land, for a more sedentary life. The nomads are already having some difficulty accepting these inevitable new forms of lifestyle. Many feel that they are perpetual prisoners of an annual climatic and vegetational cycle. If Africa is to save its savannas, several steps must be taken by the respective African governments to ensure that the pastoralists are fully aware of the adjustments toward a more sedentary life that must be made in order to preserve their culture and the environment. The pastoralists must see in education a path to enhance their productivity. Probably what should be done, as suggested by Cobern (1983), is to establish small reservations that could be helpful in the education of the nomads. In other instances mobile education systems could be set up. However, Cobern admits that in attempting to educate the nomads through these methods, the organizers of such schemes are bound to face the problems of relocation and settlement of camps and the unwillingness of educators to be involved in mobile schools.

The discovery of mineral resources in some African nations can be seen as a blessing and a curse. It is a blessing in that it gives the African nations an opportunity to participate in world trade, and in so doing enables them to obtain the necessary buying power to purchase the necessary technology for development. It is a curse in that after the discovery of natural resources such as petroleum, some African nations neglected the agricultural sector of the economy. The result is that a large percentage of the food crops, such as grain, is being imported from outside the continent. Nigeria is an example of a country that is currently suffering from the neglect of the agricultural sector. This African nation had food surpluses three decades ago, but in the 1970s and 1980s, about 70 to 80 percent of the food crop was imported (West Africa 1985).

The large number of people migrating to the African urban centers, cities, and towns poses a great problem to the planners and leaders of the countries. In an attempt to respond quickly to the problem, there have been mismanagement of the resources and errors in the planning of the infrastructures. For example, the construction of roads has been carried out without adequate planning for their maintenance and systematic coordination of the planning strategies. It is not uncommon to find that many African roads have potholes that are filled with standing water during the rainy seasons. These potholes are breeding grounds for mosquitoes (female Anopheles) that carry the parasite for the deadly malarial fever. The streets of Lagos, Nigeria, for example, have too many cars, making travel a laborious experience because of traffic congestion. Housing in the urban centers is another area where attention must be given. There is inadequate housing in the urban centers.

Educated Africans have developed appetites for Western-style housing, and in places where housing has Western-style facilities, there is a tendency for the buildings to be poorly maintained because of the lack of spare parts for repairs and in some cases the lack of technical expertise to maintain them properly. In some capital cities where multistory buildings have been built, the elevators break down frequently, and with the unreliability of electricity, the construction of such facilities is questionable. When the buildings are not properly maintained, very soon they become dilapidated.

The new population in the urban center is usually faced with the problems of unemployment and lack of proper housing. Some manage to find dwellings in rooming houses, but the average number of persons per room can be as many as four, making housing conditions deplorable. Slums and squatters can be found in many urban centers. The Lagos Eko Bridge was once a haven for homeless people. Some of these people were from neighboring West African countries. The overcrowding problem in urban housing is a subject of great debate among urban planners in Africa. Many proposals have been suggested for possible solutions to this problem, but implementing regulations on how many people can live in a house, an apartment, or a room is difficult. The open gutters of some African urban centers pose great health hazards to the public because, in many cases, they are usually clogged for weeks and sometimes for months. The stench from open gutters is not only disturbing but can be hazardous to the health of children who play close to these public health problem sites.

In sum, urban decay is caused by overcrowding, unemployment, deteriorating housing conditions, and lack of proper maintenance of infrastructures such as roads, telecommunication, and public facilities. In order to improve the quality of life of the residents, the process of urban degradation must be reversed by taking the following steps: (1) Resources should be allocated not just to urban centers but to rural communities so that the trend of migration from rural to urban settings can be stabilized. This simply means that decentralization is needed to distribute the resources in an equitable manner. Rural residents do not have to relocate to the cities in order to be gainfully employed. (2) Overcrowding can be overcome if the governments work closely with property owners (landlords) to offer reasonable rents for rooms, apartments, and houses. While private entrepreneurs should be encouraged to provide affordable housing, the governments must encourage individual people to build their own houses by providing low interest loans. Building materials must be produced locally in large quantities; importation of such materials should be discouraged, and the housing should meet the African standards. When building materials are produced locally, the maintenance of the buildings can be done at low cost and in less time. Urban and town planners should work out methods for revitalizing the urban centers.

Rural degradation is a subject of great concern to the resource planners and policymakers of African countries. Forest fires pose a great threat to the resources of the savannas and the tropical rain forests. James (1987a) reports that bush fires started by farmers have led to an increase in soil erosion and deforestation. In the last five years, thousands of acres of cultivated land in the Ivory Coast, Ghana, Togo, and Benin have been destroyed. In 1983, the late rains, coupled with dry harmattan winds from the northeastern part of the continent, exacerbated the process of vegetation destruction. Forest fires, when followed by intensive cultivation, destroy the land beyond reasonable repair. This is the case with many farmlands in Africa. If these fires are used more frequently, as is already being done in some places, there will be a gradual conversion of forests to savannas and eventually savannas to deserts. As was mentioned in an earlier chapter, the northern fringes of the Sahel are gradually becoming desert due to cattle raising and fires. People, animals, and crops suffer from such destruction. The disappearing forests of Africa are also the result of demand from the construction industry and furniture makers. For example, in Nigeria, the demand for wood products, such as sawn timber, plywood, and particle board, was more than 2 million cubic meters in 1983. The Nigerian rain forest provides more than 5 million cubic meters of logs a year. This is unquestionably one of the reasons for the gradual disappearance of African forests. The timber industry in Nigeria is not thriving as it has in the past. Already the sawmills and plymills are not being utilized to their fullest capacity. The indication from experts is that the reserved forest area in Nigeria is incapable of providing timber and log at the pace at which the demand is accelerating. Current shortages are the direct result of illegal felling and cutting down of trees over several decades. Other statistics from Nigeria show that in 1965 there were over 7 million acres of unreserved rain forests, but in 1985 there were only 963,690 acres. Efforts are being put into increasing the number of timber plantations in Nigeria, but unfortunately most of what is grown is earmarked for specific purposes. Whatever is left can be used only after these purposes have been satisfied. It was projected that from 1986 onward the Nigerian forest would be able to provide only 750,000 cubic meters of logs (*West Africa* 1985).

Other countries that should be mentioned in terms of their forest resources are the Congo, Ghana, and the Ivory Coast. Forest resources represent the second export of the Congo. The Congo can continue to enjoy the benefits of its forest resources in perpetuity if the resources are not abused and mismanaged. The Congo adopted several strategies that enabled its forest management program to succeed. The government's major objective has been to increase the number of acres of timber trees. In order to achieve this goal, over 20,000 acres of eucalyptus plantations have been established. The eucalyptus trees are a fast-growing species that attain maturity in about six to eight years. The short maturation period is good for the replenishing of the felled timber. The paper and pulp industry should be able to thrive successfully in the Congo because of the government's program.

With the assistance of the United Nations committee on Trade and Agricultural Development, an International Tropical Timber Agreement (ITTA) has been set up to operate through the International Tropical Timber Organization (ITTO). This strategy is now enabling the African countries as well as other timber-producing developing nations to participate intensely in the monitoring and regulation of timber trade. This new initiative has been instrumental in bringing the processing of tropical timber to the countries where the timber is produced. Although some West African countries, such as Ghana, envisage a bright future for their timber industries, others, such as the Ivory Coast, with its dwindling forests, anticipate hard times for the timber industry. Those countries currently experiencing decline in their timber production are taking the necessary corrective measures. Several steps are needed to reverse this trend. The felling of timber must be controlled by the local and national governments. In the Ivory Coast, for example, about 741,300 acres of forest are being destroyed in a single year; thus, protection has to be provided. In many African countries, migrant farmers are partly guilty for the damage done to the forest. Uncontrolled felling has led to the enormous reduction of traditional redwoods, leaving only secondary whitewood species. The priority for governments should be in the areas of preservation and conservation of the forests.

FOOD CRISIS IN AFRICA

In the 1950s, many African states produced enough food for themselves and were well known for their food-exporting capabilities. The situation has changed for many of these countries; in the 1970s and 1980s they have been able to survive only through the import of food and emergency food aid provided by the industrialized nations, international agencies such as the Food and Agriculture Organization (FAO), and some Arab nations. Agricultural production has declined at an alarming rate. The rising populations, economic and political problems, and drought have exacerbated the food crisis in the African countries. The whole world had to respond to the continent's widespread famine in 1983 in order to save human lives. Many African nations have become dependent on imported food products because of the failure of agriculture and the environmental crisis that have plagued the continent in the last two decades.

The impact of agricultural failure becomes obvious when one examines statistics published by the Food and Agriculture Organization of the United Nations. It is estimated that about 7.2 million people faced starvation during the 1983 food crisis. The plummeting of cereal production was not the only agricultural problem. Abnormal weather patterns disrupted crop production during the drought period. There were long dry seasons along the coastal regions of West Africa, and the lingering effects of the harmattan made agricultural production almost impossible in the West African states.

The Northern Islands' drought of 1981 and 1982 led to a crop shortfall in those places. Ethiopia, which is the third most populous country in Africa, suffered a great loss in terms of food shortages and in the number of people who died from starvation. Sub-Saharan Africa became very dependent upon grain import in order to meet local demand. Unfortunately, many of the African governments are experiencing serious economic difficulties. The devaluation of their monies has made food import more expensive, and the capacity to purchase food products is made worse by the lack of hard currency (foreign exchange). The worsening economic problems translate into political instability.

EXTERNAL FACTORS

The International Monetary Fund (IMF) of the World Bank has been attempting to work with the African countries as well as the rest of the developing world to rectify the economic catastrophes in these countries. Assistance has been in the form of providing money for development projects, rescheduling old debts, and, when necessary, arranging new loans to enable major debtor countries to continue to service their debts. The World Bank operates in this way to avert major default by the debtor countries, since such default could destabilize the international financial system. There are several arguments that the loans do not and will not solve the development problems of Africa, that these loans are by nature designed to keep the developing countries perpetually dependent upon the Western nations. It is difficult to make such an indictment at this time, although the aim of much of the assistance from the World Bank is to provide more loans to debtor countries that agree to the IMF-approved policy reforms in the tradition of the Western economies. The policies do not generally enhance economic progress or solve the developing state's problems. For instance, although the loan may increase productivity, the debt service charges on the loans seem to rise at a faster rate, and thus an increasing proportion of the foreign exchange earnings have to be used to pay the service charges. The African economic situation is alarming; the continent is experiencing serious problems, which seem to be mounting year after year. The total debt for all African countries by 1985 was $158 billion. The World Bank statistics indicate that Africa's debt service increased from $14.9 billion in 1983 to $18.9 billion in 1984. In 1985, it was in excess of $20 billion; unfortunately, this amount represents about 25 percent of the total export earnings for the whole continent (World Bank 1985a).

Since the developing nations have become dependent on the Western countries for their development, the IMF has a great influence on the economic policies of these countries. Acceptance of loans means that the projects these countries are to carry out must have some approval from the IMF; thus, economic programs are formulated in the image of the IMF. Even countries that have resisted the enticement of loans can still feel the impact of IMF on their economic policies, because as long as the development programs initiated by an African government demand the participation of a Western nation, the IMF's influence will be felt. Angola is one of the few countries that have been reluctant to seek the assistance of the IMF. The officials of this south African country contend that increasing foreign debt does not necessarily mean progress but instead means that developing nations will become more and more dependent on developed countries. They envisage that developing countries can only escape the serious economic dilemma by managing their resources properly and exporting them for revenue.

Many developing countries have been having difficulties paying back their loans. Some have had to stop ongoing projects because of budgetary problems. Several suggestions have been proposed by African countries on how to repay their loans. One such plausible suggestion was put forward by the Nigerian head of state, Babangida, who contends that repayment of loans should be limited to the amount the debtor country can afford (*West Africa* 1986). Unfortunately for the debtor nations, the IMF argues that debtor countries must accept Western terms in order to have the client relationship. It appears that African economies, which are being created by IMF standards, are not necessarily in the best interest of Africans. It is quite possible that these loans could be around indefinitely based on the current conditions and trends.

COST-BENEFIT ANALYSIS

Several benefits can be achieved by managing African resources properly. Among these are economic, aesthetic, recreational, and developmental benefits, but these must be gained at a cost that African governments can afford without going into perpetual debt. Trade-offs will have to be made in order to adequately tap the benefits of the resources.

Individual governments have begun efforts to achieve self-sufficiency in food production. In order to combat the food production problem in Nigeria, its federal government in 1980 designed a food production plan. The agricultural output of this West African country has been steadily declining for approximately twenty-one years. This decline was estimated to be about 0.4 percent in the 1960s and about 1.5 percent in the 1970s; it was probably higher in the 1980s.

The failure in agriculture has resulted from a number of factors, as previously mentioned. For example, the discovery of oil caused the federal government of Nigeria to change its priority to the development of the petroleum industry. The oil revenues of the 1960s and 1970s enabled the country to devote more energy to urban infrastructure development. Unfortunately, the urban centers became very attractive to the rural population, predominantly small-scale farmers. The net result was a reduction in the farm population. A second discouraging factor to farmers was the low prices that they were receiving for their produce. The third problem was poor access to markets. Generally, African farmers respond positively to the availability of markets. The fourth problem encountered by Nigerian farmers was bad transportation systems. The conditions of the roads are very bad, especially during the rainy season. It is usually a heavy burden to travel from one village to another, let alone from the rural communities to the urban centers. These four problems made farming very unattractive to the Nigerian people.

The federal government of Nigeria instituted the Food Strategy Mission, which established village and town markets, in order to ameliorate the farmer's plight. State governments also became involved in rebuilding existing markets in urban centers and in providing better sanitary conditions. Processing facilities, storage facilities, and better roads were constructed. These were positive incentives to small farmers.

There is one major issue at the center of agricultural systems in Nigeria and in all of Africa—the traditional system of land tenure. The small-scale farmers have holdings of fragmented lands that are not theirs. These farmers are very reluctant to develop the land to its full capacity because of their impermanency on the piece of land. The Nigerian land tenure system needs reform in order to encourage smaller farmers to dedicate themselves to the goal of developing the land. In 1978, the military government enacted a Land Use Decree, which essentially gives the government the power to reform the land tenure system. However, the government is very careful with this power. Reforms have not been introduced as aggressively as in Northern Ghana. Experience in Ghana showed that such a sudden change in land tenure can result in cultural and social problems and eventually in the political instability of a nation.

The establishment of large-scale farms are needed in order to produce enough food to feed the growing population. In the 1980s there were plans by the Nigerian government to acquire 14,000 acres of land in each of its states to be used for the production of grain. Assistance is being provided by some foreign companies. The Department or Ministry of Environment should ensure that this venture does not lead to the deterioration of the Nigerian ecosystem and result in a clash between the traditional agricultural systems (e.g., pastoralism) and the mechanized agricultural system that is being introduced to these acquired lands.

In Kenya, the introduction of mechanized agriculture led to the collapse of the traditional culture of some farmers, and the farmlands suffered tremendously from soil erosion. Foreign companies must educate their agriculturalists and engineers about the implications of transfer of agricultural technology. Though crop yield may be plentiful initially, the long-range effect of mechanized agriculture in Africa without careful study of local soil, rain patterns, and ecology could be disastrous.

Africans have always lived in harmony with the land, and spiritual links with nature are common throughout the continent. The Nigerian government has now recognized that when given the security of land tenure and ownership, farmers are more willing to put effort into the development of land.

Efforts are also being made toward making loans available to rural farmers. There is no doubt that the abuse of such a system has already taken place, whereby farmers get the loan but use it for other purposes. Nigeria and other nations where such abuse is taking place should emulate the methods instituted by Tanzania. In this method of loan distribution, the farmer who fails to show progress in crop production does not receive any other assistance from the government. The credit must be made available in rural areas by setting up rural headquarters. The Nigerian Agricultural Credit Scheme must be developed with sufficient sophistication to address rural issues.

Since the discovery of oil in Nigeria, the federal government's attention has shifted from agricultural production to oil production. Even many Nigerians who depended on subsistence agriculture for their livelihood wanted their children to leave the rural communities for urban centers, where it was generally believed that oil monies were generating job opportunities. Thus, Nigerian agriculture faced the serious problem of neglect while the population was steadily increasing.

An examination of the federal government's efforts in terms of policies and monies allocated for agricultural development indicates that adequate emphasis was not placed on increasing Nigerian agricultural products. Probably the most appropriate way to begin this investigation is to examine the amount of money spent on agriculture. It is generally true that agricultural problems impact the lives of all the citizens of any country facing the crisis. The failure of agriculture disrupts the socioeconomic and political systems.

The federal government of Nigeria did not increase its expenditure on agricultural production in the 1970s. Rupely (1980) claims that although agricultural expenditures by state governments were about 18 percent of their capital expenditures for 1975 to 1977, the federal government's expenditure on agriculture did not exceed 3 percent of the recurrent budget since 1960. Further investigation of Nigeria's budget indicates that agricultural expenditures have not exceeded 2 percent since 1975.

Despite the future threat to agriculture in Nigeria due to the diminishing resource base, the 1980 budget showed that agriculture expenditure was less than 3 percent of the total federal government expenditure. Concern about the practice of sustainable agriculture in Nigeria stems from the lack of sufficient money for research, education, incentives, and appropriate technology. The reality of limited agricultural resources has finally arrived in full force in Nigeria, as well as in many other African countries. The ramifications can be felt in the price increase in food items, as well as in other necessary commodities throughout the country. In order to have a sustained agriculture in a developing country such as Nigeria, there has to be, as Rupey (1980:1290) succinctly puts it, "considerable recurrent expenditures because the provision of inputs, extension, advice and maintenance are annual recurring items."

Angola is another country where government efforts are showing signs of improvement. The flight of the European population from Angola has meant the loss of agricultural skills. The civil unrest of the past has its beginnings in agricultural and industrial problems. Angola's economic problems reach deep into the agricultural sector. The challenge for Angola is not only to find political stability but also to balance political stability with economic and agricultural stabilities. Like many African nations, Angola realizes that it cannot feed its population. Thus, foreign assistance is required to meet the demand for food.

Despite the political and economic problems plaguing Angola, it seems to be one of the few African countries making tremendous progress toward self-sufficiency. Many projects have begun in order to combat the problem of agricultural failure. Research by Foy (1980) discusses how the government has set up provincial headquarters to handle the planning and development of the different agricultural sectors. Although the departure of the Europeans has stagnated the production of food crops in Angola, efforts are under way to reverse the situation. The government has set production goals agreed upon by management and farmers' representatives, and the Ministry of Agriculture is to ensure that these goals and objectives are included in the agricultural development plans. A systematic approach to resource management has been instituted in this African nation to coordinate state farms with transportation systems. Such a system will enhance food distribution and the export of cash crops. Despite the year-long civil war, invasion from South Africa, and refugee problems, Angolan agriculture seems to be facing a bright future.

Senegal, like Burkina Faso, Niger, Sudan, and Ethiopia, has been experiencing drought problems. The effect of drought has increased the problem of food production in Senegal. In 1980, Senegal suffered an extended period without rain. When the rain finally came, it was too much, which led to the destruction of livestock; cattle were infected with diseases, and planting was made difficult. One of the problems that many African countries like Senegal have to resolve is what can be done under such conditions. The government and people should be ready to deal with such circumstances, which require advance planning to avoid widespread hunger and the displacement of human population.

The 1980 drought affected the Senegalese economy in a negative way because about one-half of Senegalese export is agricultural products. Export crops such as groundnut were severely damaged, and, of course, people whose employment was associated with export crops were economically disadvantaged. International assistance had been on a steady decline since the 1980s, so the government of Senegal had to reevaluate its needs. Many industrial endeavors had to be put on hold in order to feed the country. The situation that came about as a result of the drought brought the government to the hard reality that agricultural policies must recognize the possibilities of catastrophes such as drought. The government is currently planning for sustainable agriculture so that the citizens of the country will always have food irrespective of meteorological conditions. The program is already in place, but the specifics are not yet detailed in any public documentation. In order to stop the destruction of livestock in the event of drought, the government is making feedlots available at very cheap prices so that rural farmers can purchase them. The programs of reforestation and dam construction that have already begun will also help in the future to diminish problems associated with drought.

Ghana's effort to increase food production is commendable because it recognizes the significance of training indigenous people in techniques of modern agriculture suitable to the Ghanaian environment. In this endeavor, an international and interuniversity venture was embarked upon by Ghanaian and Canadian universities in the early 1970s. The effort between the universities in the two countries meant training Ghanaians in fields such as nutrition, soil science, and agriculture. Fellowships were awarded to Ghanaians to study in Canadian universities, and upon completion of their education, they brought back the acquired and appropriate knowledge to Ghana. Research that was pertinent to Ghanaian soils, crops, and other agriculturally related areas were conducted by the participants in the venture. This program, which continued into the 1980s, was successful because the studies were useful to agricultural improvement in

Ghana. This success could be emulated by other African countries (*West Africa* 1980).

In order to combat the problem, African countries have been receiving assistance in producing food. The United Nations Development Program (UNDP) in 1981 began investigating ways of assisting West African nations in developing their river basins. In some cases, international agencies have cooperated or are in the process of finalizing plans on how to work together in order to improve the human conditions in Africa. For example, in West Africa, the United Nations Environmental Program (UNEP) and the UNDP launched a $10 million project in 1981 to assist the Guinean government in developing its water resources. These two agencies have sought assistance for developing countries from developed nations. In 1979, ten African countries were affected by drought, while in 1981, thirty African countries were affected, twenty of them seriously. If the effects of such catastrophes are to be ameliorated, the resources of African rivers must be developed to their fullest potential. There is definitely an urgent need to develop African water resources.

Most experts agree that progress being made is insufficient to ensure that the effects of future droughts are not as serious as they have been in the past. However, since 1981, several plans have been made. The UNDP has launched a $60 million energy fund to assist developing countries in energy-related problems. Africa has received a substantial percentage of that amount.

The UNDP has also started industrialization of the Third World countries. The aim is to encourage indigenous industries with strong participation of peoples native to the countries where the industries are being established. By 1981, the UNDP was supporting about 1,580 industrialization projects in the developing countries. It is estimated that one-third of that total was in Africa, to enhance the wise use of resources by African people, the United Nations Decade for Transport in Africa (1978–87) has enabled many African nations to participate in the management of their resources. While improving the quality of life of many millions of people, transportation systems will also enhance the preservation and conservation of resources. It is estimated that of the 111 resident representatives of the UNDP, about 45 are based in Africa to report on the progress being made in natural resource development, technological development, and education (Madeley 1980).

Mali's economic problem is exacerbated by drought and the food deficit. In 1980, food crops—millet, maize, and sorghum—fell to 950,000 tons from 1,060,000 tons in 1978–79. Groundnut production fell from 125,000 tons in 1980 to 109,000 tons in 1981. Paddy rice fell from 250,000 tons in 1980 to 185,000 tons in 1981. The trade deficit is staggering. In 1980, France's aid to that country was cancelled; hence, Mali must put a greater emphasis on developing its natural resources so that it can be self-sufficient in the next decade or two. Urgent steps must be taken to develop the potential of rivers, such as the Niger and the Senegal, that pass through the country. Researchers claim that the central Niger Delta has potentially 1 million acres of land that can be cultivated. Of this, only 148,260 acres are currently being utilized (*West Africa* 1980).

In order to appreciate the need for proper resource management, one must examine what happened in Mali or the Sahel countries in 1980. Famine was widespread and in some cases lingered into 1986 and will continue into the year 2000 unless drastic measures are taken. In 1980, many of the rivers, streams, and ponds in the Sahel countries dried up and resulted in the deterioration of the grazing land. Cattle were dying by the hundreds from hunger and lack of water.

In 1973, the Sahel suffered a similar situation. Many of the governments and people of the Sahel would like to contain the problems brought about by drought; thus, the need for long-range disaster planning. The heads of state of the Sahelian countries have held meetings to find solutions to their common problem. Such a meeting took place in January 1980; one of the conclusions reached was that there is a need to tap the hydroagricultural potential available in many of these countries.

ECONOMIC REALITY

Developing African nations are facing serious economic difficulties that will continue to impede their development progress. These difficulties have their origins in domestic and international policies. Domestic obstacles have emanated from political instability, mismanagement, and natural catastrophes. International policies create obstacles because the external debt problem has almost paralyzed progress in some parts of Africa and other developing countries. Thus, there is urgent need for a strategy to manage Africa's resources. Given the situation of 1984, when twenty-one African countries had serious food shortages that cost thousands of human lives, the governments of African nations are searching for long-range solutions to the problems of resource deterioration.

Since many development projects in Africa have external financial or technical support, foreign debt has been one of the major obstacles that most African nations have to overcome in order to address the issue of development adequately. It appears that in an attempt to pay back foreign loans, or at least the service charges, many developing nations have had to resort to austerity measures that seem to stagnate their progress toward attaining higher standards of living for their citizens. Many African countries, like other developing countries, have had difficulties rescheduling their loans, and many developing countries are engaged in debt accumulations to carry out their projects. Such endeavors are associated with increased debt service obligation. It stands to reason that the cycle of indebtedness will continue to leave the developing countries with a debt management crisis. African nations have shown little progress in food production output. Industrial productivity is also very slight. On the average, there has been a decline in the gross domestic product (GDP) in Africa between 1975 and 1983. The financial problems facing many African nations is compounded by commercial debts equivalent to twelve months' export earnings. Many of these nations have lost a substantial amount of export earnings.

Africa's problems can further be seen in the international export/ import trade of both natural and industrial materials. There was a 4.8 percent decline in exports by African countries in 1985. This amounted to $71.7 billion (United Nations, 1986). During the same year (1985), it was reported that Africa's imports declined by $10 billion. Overall, Sub-Saharan Africa recorded a stagnation in exports at the level of $27.2 billion, while its imports plummeted by 8 percent in 1985.

There is no doubt that when faced with serious problems, policymakers can make decisions that can result in the progress of nations. This is evident in the improvement of the trade deficit of Sub-Saharan Africa in 1985.

If African nations are to succeed in their efforts to manage their resources adequately, there must be a genuine attempt by the developed nations to cooperate in good faith. New international trade organizations should be set up to assist developing African countries. Changes requested by developing countries must be made in the world economic order, through changes in institutional systems of the world such as the General Assembly and the General Assembly's committees of the United Nations.

7   RIVER SYSTEMS OF AFRICA

With the intensification of activities involving African rivers, changes will no doubt occur. A brief look at current patterns of river use will be helpful in anticipating what might happen in the future with improved technical, managerial, and leadership skills in Africa. In this chapter the effect of major development projects on the African river ecosystem is investigated, with a focus on the roles of the four major rivers of Africa—the Nile, the Niger, the Congo, and the Zambezi (Figure 16).

This is not to suggest that the tributaries of these rivers or other smaller rivers do not play significant roles in the development of the continent. As a matter of fact, more than 60 percent of the water supply in Africa comes from small bodies of water. Many of the small rivers, such as the Volta (Ghana), the Benue (Nigeria), the Gambia (Gambia), and the Senegal (Senegal), serve the countries through which they flow in many capacities. Like the major rivers, the small rivers function as transportation corridors. Some are used for hydroelectric purposes; many of the rivers are exploited for their rich food resources and recreational use.

As a link in the hydrologic cycle, a river serves several purposes: (1) as the focal point of erosion, (2) as a transportation agent, (3) as a depository for soluble and suspended material, and (4) as a medium for the distribution of energy.

In Africa, rivers are of enormous significance to development, and for this reason their ecosystems must be protected. The ecological balance of the river shores and basins is very important to the continuous production of flora and fauna. Harnessing the river for its resources means developing the river system through a modification method. Modification of river systems is carried out through development projects in Africa.

Figure 16
Important African Rivers

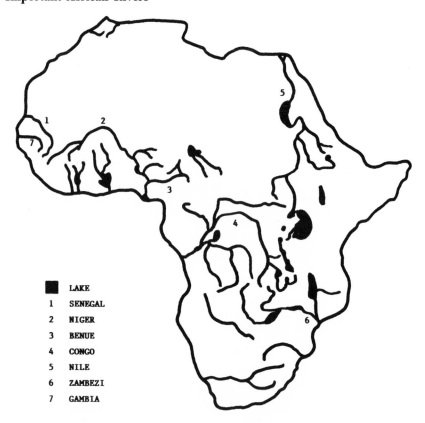

LAKE
1   SENEGAL
2   NIGER
3   BENUE
4   CONGO
5   NILE
6   ZAMBEZI
7   GAMBIA

THE NILE

The Nile drains the northeastern sector of the African continent. Its basin stretches across many climatic zones from its origin around Lakes Tanganyika, Victoria, Kyoga, Albert, Edward, George, and Rudolf to the Mediterranean Sea on the north coast of Africa (Figure 17). The southernmost source of the Nile river is just ahead of the Kogera River, as shown in Figure 17. The Nile, which played a significant role in the development of early civilizations, has a long history of being utilized for several purposes. As far back as 3000 B.C. the Egyptians have harnessed its resources. With a length of about 6,695 kilometers (4,160 miles), it prevails as the world's second longest river (Hammerton 1972). The predominant features of the Nile are shown in Figure 17. Since a more detailed description of the physical features of the Nile has been done by several

Figure 17
The Nile and Its Basin

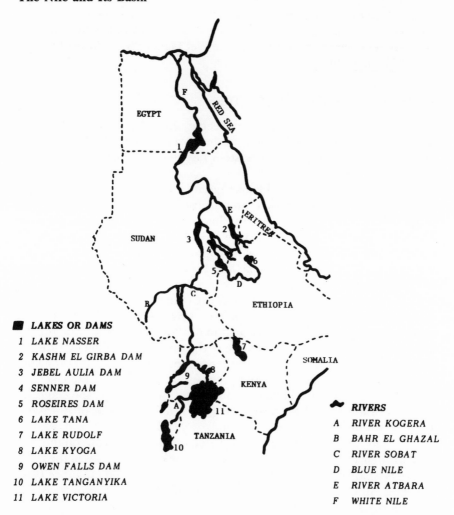

LAKES OR DAMS
1 LAKE NASSER
2 KASHM EL GIRBA DAM
3 JEBEL AULIA DAM
4 SENNER DAM
5 ROSEIRES DAM
6 LAKE TANA
7 LAKE RUDOLF
8 LAKE KYOGA
9 OWEN FALLS DAM
10 LAKE TANGANYIKA
11 LAKE VICTORIA

RIVERS
A RIVER KOGERA
B BAHR EL GHAZAL
C RIVER SOBAT
D BLUE NILE
E RIVER ATBARA
F WHITE NILE

writers, a brief description should suffice in this chapter. The White Nile, which has its origins at the head of the Luvironza River in Burindi, consists of the Victoria Nile, the Albert Nile, Bahr El Jabel, and Bahr El Abiad. The Kogera, which is Lake Victoria's main tributary, joins the White Nile at the southernmost source. There is an abundance of fish in the Nile basin, which contains about 54 genera of fish fauna, accounting for about three hundred species. The enormous amount of fish serve as food not only to the indigenous people that live close to the river but also to city dwellers. The biological diversity of the Nile is very rich. The Nile and its tributaries, like other African rivers, have a high productivity. High tropical temperatures accelerate the rate of production of phytoplankton and 300 types of zooplanktons. These in turn serve as food for the fish. The fishing industry has thrived successfully in the Nile, and experts contend that the industry has not yet been fully exploited by Africans (Hickling 1961).

HUMAN IMPACT ON THE NILE

Although human influence is noticeable, the Nile, in comparison with rivers in the industrialized nations of the world, has been fairly well maintained. Thus, although the ecosystem has changed, changes have been minimal.

On the Nile, pollution problems caused by industrialization are minor. As a source of water for irrigation purposes, the water utilized for such purposes is not returned to the river, hence reducing pollution from fertilizers. However, the Upper Nile (the Lake Victoria region) is polluted by sewage that comes from the growing population in that area. The increasing population in Kenya, Uganda, and Ethiopia will continue to increase sewage pollution on the Nile.

Dams have been constructed in order to control the flow of the Nile for the purposes of irrigation, development of hydroelectric power schemes, and the water supply. The construction of these dams were done for the most part without careful assessment of the overall environmental and socioeconomic impacts. Present experience seems to indicate that the construction of dams causes (1) rapid soil erosion, (2) silting of the lakes, (3) wildlife destruction, (4) human displacement, with demographic and social ramifications, and (5) health problems such as spread of diseases.

Early studies conducted by Monakov (1968), Talling and Rzoska (1967), and Abdin (1948) have clearly documented that dams on the Nile have influenced the steady increase in the plankton life forms in the river. There is a varying amount of zooplankton with increasing distance from the Jebel Aulia dam. The amount of zoobenthos in the river decreases as one approaches the dam.

Damming a river endangers the health of inhabitants close to the dam. Dams have led to the increase of insect pests in the Nile. In the Sudan (Khartoum), irrigation projects made possible through the construction of the Sennan dam led to an increase in chironomid midges (genus Tanytansus), which can cause asthma. Mosquitoes can also thrive in areas of close proximity to the dammed part of the river. Malarial fever is caused by the bite of the female Anopheles mosquito. The dams have, however, increased the agricultural potential of Egypt's agricultural communities. Whether the ecological disturbance outweighs the benefits of the dams has to be completely investigated in a benefit-cost analysis. Ecological repercussions, such as the endangerment of reclamation projects, the destruction of sardine fishery in the Nile delta, the spread of schistosomiasis in the irrigated areas of many dams in the Nile basin, and the silting problem, are consequences of dams on the Nile.

THE NIGER RIVER SYSTEM

It is thought that the Niger was formed from two sources. The lower southeastern part of the river was formed from the southern slopes of the Ahaggar mountains. The Sokoto and Benue Rivers in Nigeria are tributaries of the Niger that help in draining the basin (Figure 18). The Upper Niger, which flows in a northeastern direction, has its source on the Guinea–Sierra Leone border. African rivers have some fish species that are common to all of them because the rivers have a linkage in their early historical formation (Beadle 1974), but the Niger River is unique in that the lower, middle, and upper sections have different characteristics.

The Upper Niger is located in an area of Africa with plenty of rainfall. This area has been reported to show occasional flooding. However, it is important to mention that this portion of the Niger River is prone to ecological disturbance due to the unpredictable weather conditions. In Bamako (Guinea) the river debouches onto a gentle gradient and covers the swampy flood plain. The Lower Niger flows rather gently through the countries Burkina Faso and Nigeria. The Niger could thus be described as originating from the Fouta Jallon Mountain with a rapidly spreading upper section, and then spreading out over an immense middle section consisting of flood plains at high water. The river finally shrinks into a narrow river at low water, leaving small lakes, several pools, and swamps that are subject to decrease in the amount of water they contain during the long, dry seasons.

Several environmental impact analyses were conducted before the construction of the Kainji Dam on the Niger River (Scudder 1966; Visser 1970; Imerbore 1967). A significant amount of clearing and burning was done to enable fishing to be carried out in the area surrounding the lake. The Kainji has enhanced the supply of electricity to many parts of Nigeria. It has had a substantial impact on the fish population and other aquatic life in the Niger. The Kainji Dam is utilized for hydroelectric power and agricultural projects, such as irrigation. The development of hydroelectric power plants on the Niger has led to the impoundment of water, which increases the quantity of water in the dam. The flora and fauna that are not able to withstand such an increase in water have been known to perish. This situation is common in all the African dams. The artificial retention of water caused by dam construction results in turbidity of the water, oxygen loss, fish kill, algal blooms, and aquatic weed, which initially are impediments to the normal functioning of the river. Agricul-

Figure 18
The Niger and Its Basin

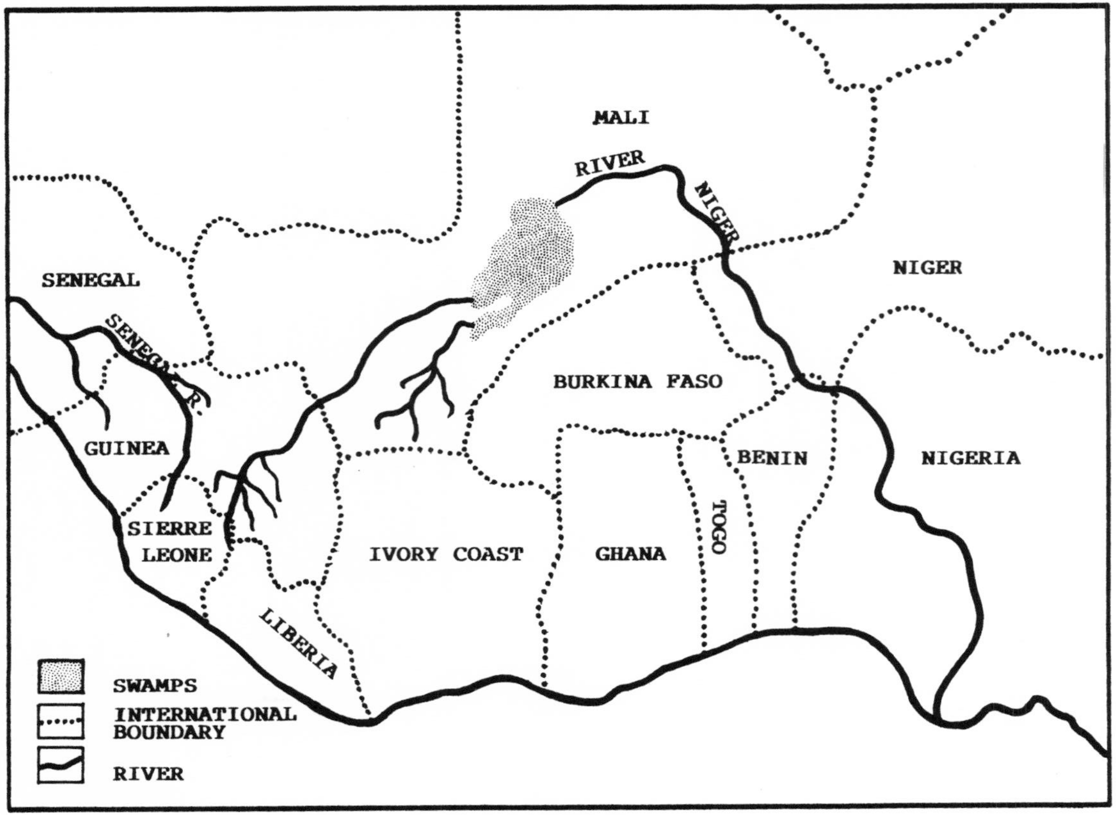

NIGER

NIGERIA

NIGER

BENIN

RIVER

BURKINA FASO

TOGO

MALI

GHANA

RIVER

IVORY COAST

LIBERIA

SENEGAL

RIVER

SIERRE
LEONE

GUINEA

SENEGAL

SWAMPS

INTERNATIONAL
BOUNDARY

RIVER

tural development projects, such as irrigation, which trigger ecological imbalance in the river ecosystems, cause problems, which vary depending on the amount of water removed. Africa's four major rivers experience some ecological disturbance due to irrigation projects. The negative effect of dams also includes an initial decrease in the number of fish and fish parasites, and the deeper sections of the lakes are usually uninhabitable by fish. However, it should be recognized that dams also assist in an increase in biological productivity of the river. Hence, the rapid increase in fish population in certain parts of the river is a direct result of the dam. The construction of the Kainji Lake had some implications on public health and the resettlement of the people around the Kainji dam.

Dam construction has resulted in the displacement of several thousands of people in Africa. The implications are usually incalculable because the projects disrupt cultural, social, and economic patterns that have taken thousands of years to evolve. The African societies must make sure that the trade-offs are worth the destruction of cultures.

Although this chapter has highlighted the negative effects of dams, it should be pointed out that African dams have had some positive socioeconomic effects on the rural populations. Such effects are especially true in the case of the irrigation projects with rivers in Nigeria.

THE RIVER CONGO

Several authors, such as Cahen (1954), have discussed the historical formation of the Congo. This river covers approximately 4 million square kilometers and drains Africa's moist tropical forest. It is believed that the Congo River system may have been in existence since the Pleistocene era. Figure 19 shows the Congo, its basin, and the associated lakes. The middle section of this river flows across the tropics in a wide and gradual meandering fashion. It is blessed with many tributaries that are rich in flora and fauna. The fish communities are numerous, and it is estimated that the entire basin (excluding Lake Tanganyika) contains 669 valid species of fish (Beadle 1974). The swamps and the lower tributaries of the Congo contain enormous amounts of flora and fauna that are not rivaled by any other river in the tropics. The biological diversity that is currently present in the Congo basin is not seriously threatened, but experience from the Amazon basin shows that restraint must be exercised when planning for river development. If the restraints are not taken seriously, the biological diversity of this great river could decline.

THE ZAMBEZI

The Congo and the Zambezi have a common watershed. This explains why the same species of fish can be found in both river systems, although

Figure 19
The Congo River

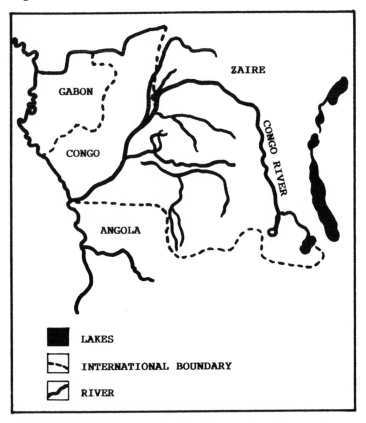

the Congo is richer in species numbers. The Zambezi is navigable by small boats. Unlike the other great African rivers, the geology of the Zambezi has been little researched. Nonetheless, the few studies that are available on the Zambezi emphasize the Kariba dam. Figure 20 shows the river system. Beadle (1974) argues that the presence of falls and rapids on the course of the Zambezi has hampered the distribution of fish in the basin. It is estimated that there are about fifty-eight species of fish in the middle section of the river, while there are about eighty-four species in the upper part of the river.

Lake Kariba (a dam) has played a significant role in the rural development of Zambia and Zimbabwe. The lake, about 300 kilometers long, with an average breadth of about 30 kilometers and a depth of about 30 meters, is located in the center of the Zambezi Valley.

The completion of the Kariba Dam was followed by a rapid increase in

Figure 20
The Zambezi River

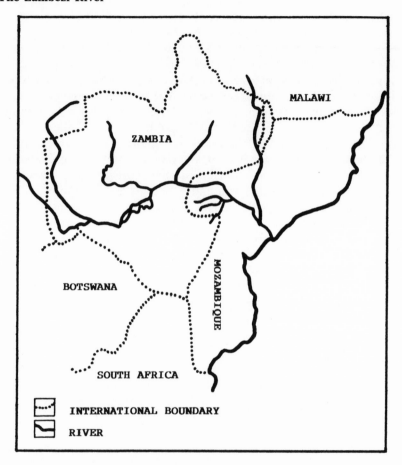

phytoplankton numbers. However, the increase in phytoplankton was temporary, and the Zambezi has recovered very well. The deoxygenation has since subsided, and fish fauna and plant life are thriving. Notwithstanding, there are still fluctuations in the water level during the dry season. Some researchers, such as Scudder (1966), have argued that the construction of large dams in Africa takes away the opportunity for a comprehensive river basin development.

CONCLUSION

The impact of human activity on African rivers has accelerated only in the last century. The rivers have supported the African ways of life with regard to agriculture, transportation, and domestic water supply. Dumping of waste (both human and industrial) is only one aspect of population growth and industrialization. The problems associated with hydroelectric power must be seriously tackled by African countries.

Several steps are being taken in order to deal with future problems. Many African universities, researchers, and international organizations are involved in research programs in Africa that can adequately address the issue of dwindling water resources in Africa. Several smaller rivers in Africa where dams have been constructed are undergoing serious monitoring. For example, the Kamburul Gtaur hydroelectric dam area in Kenya is being studied on a continuous basis in order to document its impact on the river. The Kainji Dam in Nigeria has been thoroughly studied through the efforts of international conferences organized to investigate better ways of managing the dam and its immediate environment. The work that has been done with the Nile is commendable; the more recent constructions are designed to control floods and assist agricultural output. Further and continuous research should be conducted to investigate better ways of dealing with the social and biological ramifications of river disturbance through the use of its resources.

8 AFRICA'S URBAN AND RURAL DIFFERENCES: THE CASE OF NIGERIA

Developing nations of the world are undergoing tremendous changes with regard to rapid exploitation of their natural resources, construction of infrastructure, economic development, and political instability. These changes are brought about through the gradual urbanization of rural areas, population mobility, and development in general. This chapter is an attempt to investigate the differences between the urban and rural areas of an African nation—Nigeria. Such a study raises theoretical and practical questions pertinent to the comprehensive planning efforts in developing countries. The current trends of urbanization and the decline of rural communities warrant serious examination.

Sorokin and Zimmerman (1929) concluded in their extensive theoretical study of rural and urban worlds that deep and important differences between urban and rural phenomena exist in Western cultures. Their study was essentially from a sociological standpoint, and emphasis was placed on sociological indicators. Another study was conducted by Swedner (1960) in which the ideas of Sorokin and Zimmerman were extended into the realm of stimulus response theory. The major thrust of Swedner's investigation, although it parallels Sorokin's and Zimmerman's (Figure 21), was to use empirical data available in 1957 to determine the "magnitude of urban-rural differentiation" within a selected area in southern Sweden. This chapter is an attempt to answer the question, What is the nature and magnitude of ecological differences between typical urban and rural communities in Africa?

There seems to be a general consensus among agencies concerned with development assistance that the rate and scale of urbanization poses a threat to the quality of life of the millions of people in the developing na-

Figure 21
Urban-Rural Differentiation

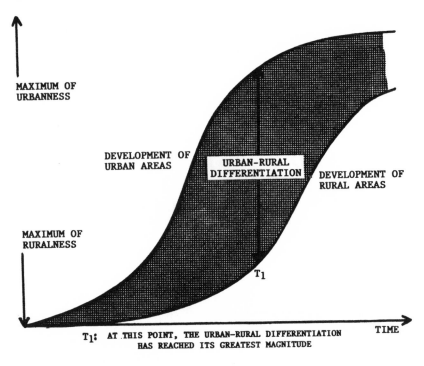

T₁: AT THIS POINT, THE URBAN-RURAL DIFFERENTIATION HAS REACHED ITS GREATEST MAGNITUDE

Source: Swedner, Harold. 1960. *Ecological Differentiation of Habits and Attitudes.* New York: CWK Gleerup/Lund: 67.

tions. Between 1975 and 1985, the developing countries of Africa almost doubled their populations. Estimates given by the United Nations Committee on Housing, Building, and Planning as early as 1969 indicate that if the developing world is to keep up with the alarming growth, the whole complex urban pattern that currently exists would have to be recreated in a couple of years.

The African situation needs careful examination, since major cities in that continent are doubling in population every decade. McNamara (1969) contends that by the year 2000, cities in the developing world will have grown by about 500 percent. In typical African cities such as Lagos (Nigeria), Nairobi (Kenya), Accra (Ghana), or Monrovia (Liberia), the problems of urbanization include (1) traffic congestion, (2) transportation inadequacies, (3) growing unemployment and underemployment, (4) housing shortage, (5) water supply problems, (6) sewage and drainage problems, and (7) deficits in social services.

Before each one of the seven problems is discussed in detail, it is important to stress the point that there is a growing awareness in Africa and abroad that the phenomenon of urbanization presents several problems that cannot be adequately addressed by using Western ideas. The problems of urbanization in Africa have arisen because the major urban centers are not well planned or adequately managed to accommodate the growth that they are facing. Although the rapid rate of urbanization in Africa is the direct result of population explosion, experts such as Feldman (1987) claim that the population of the developing nations could be declining because, on the average, women had four children in the 1980s, as opposed to six in the 1960s. Bongarts (1987:3) supports Feldman's prediction by suggesting that the 1970s will be thought of as "the beginning of the end of population explosion in the Third World."

If the trend of reduction in number of children per family continues, there is a possibility that the problem of population impact will decrease. Nonetheless, the present situation seems to suggest that migration from rural to urban centers is a common phenomenon all over the world, but, in the Third World, the impacts are drastic. The question that can then be raised is whether African countries are going to use their limited resources to develop the rural areas in order to make them conducive for human habitation. One should understand that this will entail providing the necessary infrastructures, employment centers, and social amenities. Although such an effort will demand resource conservation and preservation and wise management techniques, it will certainly bring about a demographic balance in rural/urban development.

In discussing the urban/rural development dilemma, other issues or questions surface. Some of these questions have been discussed in the developed world, but rarely within the African context. Is urbanization in Africa going to mean the disappearance of the rural communities? To what extent is the trend a threat to the ecosystems? Will rural-urban differentiation in Africa slow down with time?

Africa's population is increasing rapidly; along with the increase come changes in the urban and rural environments. The majority of Africans can be said to live in rural areas, although the current situation indicates that the migratory pattern in many African countries has changed from "rural to rural" to "rural to urban." In Nigeria for example, about 80 percent of the total population of about 100 million people still live in rural areas of that country (Kulshrestha and Mohammed 1984). Data collected by Obok (1980) indicates that the immigration trend in Calabar (Nigeria) is not just from urban to urban; a greater percentage is rural to urban.

THE SCENARIO IN NIGERIA

The absence of national strategy on urbanization and regional or rural development in many African countries like Nigeria has exacerbated development and environmental problems. Since economic considerations have always guided the national plans of Third World countries, little attention has been given to environmental degradation.

Population Distribution

The population of the great African nation of Nigeria has exploded in the last three to four decades. This increase has worsened the problem of an uneven pattern of population distribution in the country, but, although there is a large population concentration in urban areas, a large percentage of Nigerians still live in the rural areas. Several studies indicate that urban areas in Africa have steadily been gaining population from the rural areas. Many of the people move to the urban centers for several reasons, which include seeking employment, need for better education, and closeness to family members. A study conducted by Obok (1980) on the relative effects of urban-rural migration in Calabar (Nigeria) shows that in 1946, the population of this town was approximately 10,000 but by 1978, the population was 120,000. This is the general trend in many other urban towns in Nigeria and in Africa as a whole. The problem associated with the current migration is twofold: (1) rural environmental, economic, social, and cultural decline, and (2) urban environmental, economic, and social decline.

The rural situation will be examined first. Much theoretical research has been done in order to explain the reasons for migration from the rural areas of developing countries and to shed some light on why the degradation of the rural areas is almost impossible to stop given the current and projected economic conditions of many developing countries. Although the emphasis in this section is on rural-urban migration, it should be emphasized that rural and urban-rural migration also occur in Africa.

Research conducted by agencies of the United Nations and other independent investigators conclude that very little development has been achieved in the Third World countries. The vast majority of the population in the rural parts of Nigeria as well as other African countries remains poor.

Peil and Sada (1984) suggest that there are two opposing ideas about the influence of migration on rural communities. One view, which they call "equilibrium view," is based on the premise that surplus cash from urban areas enhances the standard of living of rural residents. The assumption is that migrants from rural areas assist other rural residents to succeed in urban areas. This viewpoint seems to suggest that migration from rural areas is economically beneficial.

The other view sees the rural communities as dependent upon other sources for their survival. This idea believes that migration from rural communities takes away revenue because of the abandonment of cash crop cultivation. It is also argued that, although raw materials are taken from the rural area, the headquarters for processing and setting policies concerning the exploitation of natural resources are usually in the urban areas, leaving the former economically and politically neglected.

Many young men and women in rural parts of Nigeria leave home for education in the cities. After obtaining their education, they eventually locate permanently in the cities. Their education is usually wholly or partly supported with resources from their rural homes. Such trends are common all over Nigeria and many parts of other African countries. The cultural influence of the urban areas on the rural areas is a well-known fact, and the villages perceive the urban value as a negative influence.

Strategies profitable for households in urban areas often deprive rural societies of resources for development and increase differentiation between rural and urban areas. The demographic effects of migration often mean a shortage of labor in rural communities. Emigration leaves the rural areas with very young and elderly people who can do very little in the development process of rural communities.

Migration deprives the village of the ability to maintain enough labor for subsistence food production and for export crops; eventually the national economy suffers, since traditional agriculture is labor intensive.

Very little development has been achieved in developing countries in comparison with the leaps and bounds that are taking place in the industrialized nations. The little development that is taking place in the rural communities has relied heavily on the exploitation of natural resources, often resulting in destruction of the rich ecosystems of the developing countries. The lack of proper management techniques, disregard for ecological equilibrium by international corporations, and lack of political will have all contributed to the dilemma that is occurring all across the Third World.

Rural planning in Nigeria has received little attention for a number of reasons. The reasons become obvious when one examines (1) the political and planning climate in the country, (2) availability and inadequacy of technical expertise of resource management, (3) environmental impact analysis before a major infrastructure project, (4) the green revolution, (5) the carrying capacity of productive land, (6) employment/unemployment, and (7) allocation of resources. These issues have either not been properly addressed or not addressed at all in some rural communities. The need to maintain ecological/biological diversity has been discussed in detail by IUCN (1980), Soule and Wilcox (1980), and Frankel and Soule (1981). Suffice it to say here that rural development projects have accelerated deforestation in Nigeria because of clearance for agriculture and other land uses. Current estimates show that the western coast of Africa, from Guinea Bissau to Nigeria, has less than 45 million hectares of forest. Many of the countries in West Africa do not have any tropical moist forest left. Expert opinions of agronomists and foresters conclude that the development approach most likely to succeed in the rural parts of Nigeria and the rest of Africa is one that incorporates or enhances the diversity and complex interdependence of the rural environment.

One of the reasons why the rural areas of Nigeria, like those of many other developing countries, are becoming economically depressed is that rural-urban migration drains the rural communities of the labor supply that is critically needed to accomplish the development programs that are initiated. Many young people leave the rural communities because they are in search of good education that would make them employable in the urban areas or because the land tenure system does not offer them opportunities to earn a decent living in the rural areas. To make matters worse, neither the government nor international assistance benefit the rural inhabitants who grow the crops and raise the goats, cattle, and sheep.

Land Use Changes in Urban and Rural Areas

The inhabitants of rural communities are the only people with the proven ability to sustain a living from the forests and savanna regions of Nigeria, but researchers have shown that such sustained living has gradually taken its toll on the natural resources as the population increased. Adeyoju (1975:18) states:

Indeed, in Nigeria man first started to destroy his natural heritage about four thousand years ago when settled farming replaced food gathering in the last Stone Age culture of Nok. These people were apparently agriculturists who also kept cattle. When the Nok culture reached its peak during the 900 B.C. to 200 B.C. on the Jos Plateau, most of the land of that area was probably still covered with high forest. What happened to the Nok people is not known, but the forests are gone, and the best examples of soil erosion in Nigeria can be found on the Jos Plateau.

The influence of firewood collection in the Nigerian forests and savannas is obvious since the majority of the people depend on firewood as a source of energy for cooking. Firewood collection coupled with clearance for agriculture and other land uses has exacerbated the deforestation process in Nigeria. Historical evidence indicates that the process of deforestation in Nigeria began with the introduction of settled agriculture due to increase in population. Malaysian food crops such as yams, rice, bananas, mangoes, coconut palm, and sugar cane were introduced into the country to feed the growing population. The average annual deforestation in Nigeria as well as other West African countries is about 4 percent. Based on the evidence of the slow destruction of forests and savanna regions of Nigeria, it is now clear that the agroecological approach most suitable for the rural areas of the country must take into account the diversity and complex interdependence of the rural environment. This approach must be considered the most appropriate because many subsistence farmers in Nigeria still believe strongly in shifting cultivation through the slash-and-burn method.

Nigerian farmers who predominantly live in the rural areas of the country occupy a unique position in the preservation of the biological diversity of that country. With the increasing disappearance of the forests and the destruction of the ecosystems, it is imperative for the Nigerian government to inform rural farmers about the threat they pose to endemic species and the ecosystem at large as a result of the farmers' migration to new rural areas. Several mechanisms for preserving biological diversity through traditional agricultural systems in Nigeria would make the preservation of the rural areas possible. For examples, dooryard gardens incorporating the use of traditional tools, are semi-intensive, and do not require intensive clearing (Myers 1984).

Allen and Barnes (1985) seem to think that the only way rural subsistence agriculturalists can increase income is to increase output. Thus the two avenues open to them are expansion and intensification. Since available land is becoming very scarce in already settled parts of Nigeria, the farmers migrate to uncultivated grasslands, shrublands, and forests. Their attempt to produce more food inevitably leads to the conversion or destruction of the forests and savannas.

Nigeria, like many other African countries, is forced by economic, social, and political problems to exploit its natural resources. Thus, the problem of environmental degradation is one that deserves immediate and worthwhile attention. The World Resources Institute in 1984 expressed the same opinion.

Culture also has an influence on the preservation of natural resources. With increases in population and urbanization, there is a gradual decline of remote cultural values in Nigeria and the rest of Africa. The Western or industrialized nations have influenced the Nigerian culture immensely. The replacement of an authentic Nigerian culture with a foreign industrial culture disregards the laws of nature and exacerbates the problems of resource abuse. But it should be emphasized that the traditional Nigerian society also produced forest and savanna destruction. The small population of the past (say two hundred years ago) and the lack of large-scale technology restricted resource abuse. But the continuous exponential increase in the population of the country poses a very serious threat to the environment. Government policies influence the environment. Unstable governments produce unstable economic structures that enact catastrophic policies that fail to protect natural resources. Unstable governments are manipulated by foreign industrialized nations for the natural resources. Nigeria has suffered tremendously as a result of its unstable governments.

In the 1980s Nigeria and the rest of Africa lost many plant and animal species due to the indiscriminate destruction of the forests. Given this loss, there should be an attempt to integrate planning and preservation due to the interlinkage of the ecosystem.

Planning questions and solutions follow from the above discussion. The first obvious question is: What kind of rural planning/development policy exists in Nigeria? Adeyoju (1975:19) suggests that the history of natural resource use and development in Nigeria dates back to colonial days.

At the end of the nineteenth century Nigeria was administered as three different territories: the Colony and Protectorate of Lagos, the Niger Coast Protectorate, previously known as the Oil Rivers Protectorate, and the more northerly country under the influence of the Royal Niger Company Limited. Organized forestry started first in the Colony and Protectorate of Lagos and owes its beginning to a Governor, Sir Alfred Moloney, whose enthusiasm was demonstrated in the publication of the *Sketch of the Forestry of West Africa* in 1887 to commemorate Queen Victoria's jubilee. Ten years later, the Acting Governor of Lagos, Sir George Denton, recommended the formation of a Forest Department, the duty of which was to protect the existing forests and draw up plans for the reforestation of denuded areas. In 1899, Cyril Punch was appointed to Lagos Colony to look after the forestry affairs while Peter Hitchens was assigned to similar duties throughout the Niger Coast Protectorate, with Calabar as his station.

CONCLUSIONS AND RECOMMENDATIONS

If rural planning is to succeed in Nigeria, the following concerns need to be taken into account: (1) Planning policy in Nigeria has been inclined toward urban planning. Rural planning policies are deficient of concrete commitment, and the net result is that what is currently available is a haphazard development that tends to neglect the laws of nature. There seems to be a lack of commitment on the part of those who are supposed to enforce the laws and regulations of the federal government to protect the rural environment. (2) The planning offices in rural communities are understaffed and have inadequate funds to conduct proper and adequate research in rural communities to enhance infrastructure construction. (3) Environmental impact statements are gradually becoming a part of development projects in Africa, but in some rural areas of Nigeria, this concept has not been taken seriously. (4) The "green revolution" that was introduced into Nigeria in the early 1980s opened the door for many subsistence farmers to try to maximize the amount of crops that they could get from the land. The lack of proper planning of that effort led to the destruction of many prime ecological settings. (5) Rural development, whether it is in the form of new industry, infrastructures, or agricultural settings, must take into account the people's lifestyle. It must address employment or unemployment and the demographic impacts of the community. (6) Above all, with the current and gradual deterioration of the Nigerian ecosystem, one of the primary ways of reversing the situation would be to conduct development with the consciousness of what the carrying capacity of the rural area is at any particular time.

9 PERCEPTIONS OF RESOURCE MANAGEMENT PROBLEMS

One of the contributing factors to the deplorable situation of poverty in Africa is the widespread loss of forests. In many parts of Africa, as in many other parts of the developing world, the less wealthy people are among the agents of the conversion and destruction of the forests. In order to produce subsistence food and provide themselves with fuelwood, they clear-cut the forests. Faced with unemployment, the rural poor attempt to survive by exploiting the natural resources—the forest. Global evidence indicates that there is a clear correlation between poverty and deforestation. Several works have indicated that the rate at which forest resources are being exploited in Nigeria poses a threat to the ecological balance of the forest region of the country. There has been a rapid decline in the forest products that the country can export.

Farmers play a significant role in the resource management of developing countries. In this chapter, an attempt is made to investigate the perception of resource management by farmers in a small town, Ikot Ekpene, in Akwa Ibom State of Nigeria (Figure 22). The study presented in this chapter concentrates on farmers because about 70 percent employment in Nigeria is related to agriculture.

THE SURVEY POPULATION

The study was conducted primarily with farmers and agriculturalists ("people who have agricultural interests") in Ikot Ekpene. Since about 85 percent of the households in Ikot Ekpene have at least one or more members of the family involved with subsistence agriculture, the researcher ap-

Figure 22
Map of Southeastern Nigeria

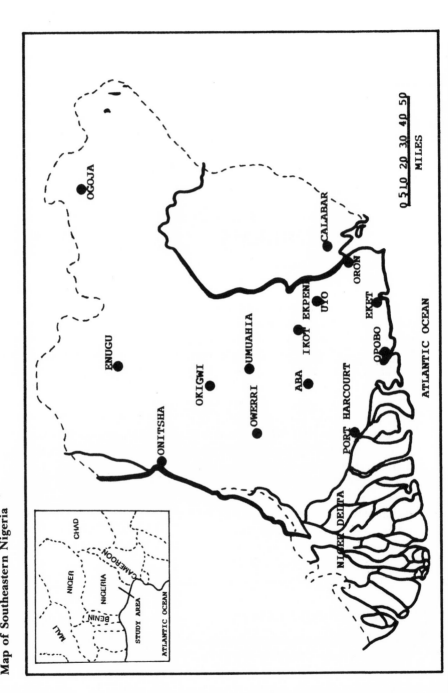

proached members of randomly selected families with farmers with the questionnaires.

THE SURVEY MATERIAL

One instrument (see Appendix) was used for the survey of the farmers. The questionnaire was necessary because it enabled the farmers to take their time with their responses. There were twenty multiple choice questions addressing resource management in terms of agriculture. The questions were grouped into four major categories: (1) causes of agricultural decline, (2) causes of deforestation and/or vegetation loss, (3) national and international policies and attitudes about environmental concern, and (4) possible agricultural policies to be adopted.

During December 1987, questionnaires were distributed to the farmers who were randomly sampled (according to households). One hundred and twenty questionnaires were distributed by hand; the author was able to obtain one hundred questionnaires three days later. Thus, the return rate was 83.3 percent.

FINDINGS

In order to plan effectively for progressive agricultural development and solutions to current and future problems, it is imperative to understand some of the reasons why Nigeria's agriculture has been on the downward trend in the past decade. With respect to Ikot Ekpene, it was necessary to ask questions concerning the causes of agricultural problems in Nigeria. Table 9 shows a summary of the responses of Ikot Ekpene farmers with respect to the causes of agricultural problems. Of the one hundred respondents, twenty of the farmers thought that there was not enough research being carried out to support their efforts.

One is led to think from the results of Item 1 that the majority of farmers of this small town do not really feel that research is absolutely necessary in order for them to produce enough food for themselves. The second item shows that 45 percent of the respondents strongly feel that managerial skills are essential for the adequate management of the natural resources. This result seems to parallel the assessment given to the researcher by some elders of the town. They contend that the gradual destruction of the natural resources indicates that it is necessary for those who utilize the natural resources, either for development purposes or for agriculture, to learn how to properly manage the natural environment.

The third item of Table 9 concerns the issue of population. In this part of Nigeria, polygamy is still prevalent; hence it was important to investigate how the respondents felt about this issue. Thirty percent of the respondents felt that checking the population would help the agricultural

Table 9

Summary of Responses of Nigerian Farmers to Questions on the Causes of Nigerian Agricultural Problems

Statement	Strongly Agree	Agree	Don't Know	Disagree	Strongly disagree
1. There is not enough research conducted to improve the quality and quantity of food production in Nigeria.	20%	30%	20%	30%	0%
2. The lack of management skills is one of the problems facing Nigeria with regard to resource management.	45%	22%	2%	21%	10%
3. Agricultural problems could be ameliorated in many parts of Nigeria if population increase is checked.	10%	20%	30%	40%	0%
4. The political instability of Nigeria exacerbates agricultural problems.	50%	20%	10%	10%	10%

situation. In private conversations with some of the people, it was revealed that the large family system makes farm work easy because labor can be readily provided.

Table 9 indicated that 50 percent of the farmers strongly feel that the political instability of the country does affect agricultural productivity.

The subject of deforestation has been discussed in detail in Chapter 2. But it should be emphasized that it is one of the greatest problems facing Africa. Faced with the enormous shortage of food and fuel wood, the African farmer is bound to do whatever it takes to survive, even while realizing the consequences of cutting down trees and burning the grass. To the farmer, it is the day-to-day survival that is crucial and not long-term planning. Past agricultural practices in many parts of Africa have also exacerbated the problems of forest loss. In many African countries, export crops are grown in the areas of the country where rainfall is sufficient in order to obtain foreign exchange to repay their foreign debt. Such practices have led to the exposure of large tracts of land to the process of erosion. Table 10 is a summary of responses of farmers in Ikot Ekpene to questions about deforestation. Item 1 of Table 10 shows that 70 percent of the farmers who responded strongly agree that agricultural practices have resulted in the destruction of the forests and savannas. In Item 2 of Table 10, one finds that 40 percent of the respondents strongly agree that logging of timber and the cutting of trees for firewood also exacerbate the process of deforestation. It is noteworthy to emphasize that in item 3, 40 percent of the respondents agree with the contention that soil degradation due to deforestation has reached alarming proportions in many parts of the country. Sixteen percent of the farmers strongly agree with this argument. Probably the fact that 24 percent of the farmers indicated that they do not know enough to answer the questions is a vivid indication that some farmers do not understand the total ramification of deforestation. Nomadic lifestyle has continued to pose a problem as populations encroach upon the land. However, when this question was posed to the respondents, 20 percent strongly agreed with the idea that nomadic pastoralism should be abandoned in order to prevent vegetation destruction, and 30 percent agreed with the suggestion (Item 4, Table 10).

The deplorable conditions of many African countries have forced international organizations, developed nations and African governments to begin to examine their policies and attitudes toward the development of Africa. Table 11 is a summary of the responses of Ikot Ekpene farmers with regard to national and international policies. Item 1 of Table 11 indicates that 60 percent of the respondents think that the government of Nigeria is doing everything possible to enhance the management of the natural resources of the country. (The figure of 60 percent is obtained by adding the percentages of "strongly agree" and "agree.") Item 2 concerns the efforts of the Nigerian government with conservation and preserva-

Table 10
Summary of Responses of Nigerian Farmers to Questions on the Causes of Deforestation and/or Vegetation Loss in Nigeria

Statement	Strongly Agree	Agree	Don't Know	Disagree	Strongly Disagree
1. Agricultural practices in Nigeria have led to the destruction of the forests and savannas.	70%	20%	5%	5%	0%
2. Present practices such as logging for timber and firewood are increasing the problem of deforestation.	40%	30%	10%	15%	5%
3. The problem of soil degradation due to deforestation has reached alarming proportions in many parts of the country.	16%	40%	24%	10%	10%
4. Nomadic pastoralism should be abandoned in order to prevent vegetation destruction.	20%	30%	30%	7%	13%

Table 11
Summary of Responses of Nigerian Farmers to Questions on National and International Policies and Attitudes

Statement	Strongly Agree	Agree	Don't Know	Disagree	Strongly Disagree
1. Nigeria is providing the necessary environment conducive for international involvement in the management of their resources.	10%	50%	20%	10%	10%
2. The Nigerian government takes the issues of conservation and preservation seriously.	40%	20%	25%	10%	5%
3. The demand for the natural resources of Nigeria in the industrialized countries encourages the exploitation of the natural resources.	70%	20%	0%	5%	5%
4. Regional and international cooperation is necessary in order to tackle the problem of resource abuse in a developing country such as Nigeria.	60%	25%	5%	5%	5%

121

tion. Forty percent of the respondents strongly agree that the government takes the issue of conservation and preservation of natural resources seriously. As a matter of fact, the researcher noticed several advertisements sponsored by the government on local television that attempt to educate the public on the importance of planting new trees and of having an ecologically balanced environment.

Item 4 of Table 11 shows that there is a clear understanding by the farmers of the significance of regional and international cooperation in solving the problem of resource destruction. Since the agricultural sector ranks very high in the Nigerian economy, a large population of the people is involved with using the land for agricultural production. Hence, it was essential to investigate some of the parameters that must be reflected in the policies on food production. The parameters as shown in Table 12 are education, large-scale food production, local food production, and alternative food production. The responses of the farmers showed that a great majority of the farmers strongly agree with the policies that encourage ecological balance and proper development and management of the natural resources.

CONCLUSIONS AND RECOMMENDATIONS

Planning used to be linked to economic gains, but Nigerian economists who stress agricultural development at all costs are beginning to understand that certain development efforts can actually lead to the degradation of the environment. The overall impression that one gets is that the peasant farmers are becoming more conscious of environmental problems and are very familiar with some of the causes. These farmers, given the right incentives, are willing to make the necessary changes that could create a better ecological balance.

The farmers, both men and women, understand the importance of their roles in the gradual and successful protection and conservation of African resources. The significance of forestry to rural development has been made understandable to farmers who have very limited knowledge of ecological balance, and many farmers are cooperating in order to enable the government to achieve its goals of not only preserving the forests but also enhancing the process of reforestation. There is an obstacle that still needs to be overcome, and that is the lack of police power to enforce the proper management and protection of the forests. This problem is compounded by the lack of institutions (federal, regional, or local) to carry out policies stipulated at the federal levels. Planning offices are absent in many towns.

Nonetheless, it does appear that with the creation of new states, many local agencies will be set up to manage the resources properly and adequately. Many local residents are now taking active roles in the manage-

Table 12

Summary of Responses of Nigerian Farmers to Questions on Possible Agricultural Policies to Be Adopted

Statement	Strongly Agree	Agree	Don't Know	Disagree	Strongly Disagree
1. Education of rural farmers on issues of ecological balance should be a top priority of the developing nations' effort to discourage biological equilibrium disturbance.	50%	30%	5%	10%	5%
2. Nigeria must embark on large-scale food production instead of depending upon subsistence agriculture.	60%	20%	2%	14%	4%
3. Nigeria should cease from depending on imported food.	70%	10%	0%	3%	17%
4. Alternative energy sources for domestic use should be aggressively pursued by developing nations (instead of using firewood).	70%	10%	5%	10%	5%

ment of their resources. There are important reasons—aesthetic, economic, and ethical—why developing nations must preserve their natural resources. The forests of Nigeria as well as those of other African nations contain numerous wild plants and animals that are beneficial to human existence. The genetic diversity is important for the maintenance and sustenance of Third World agriculture. The disappearance of the forest could make the goal of self-sufficiency impossible.

Certainly present agricultural development and population increases have negative impacts on the environment. The recognition that efforts must be coordinated to correct the resulting loss of nutrients, compaction of soils, and loss of high-quality agricultural land is essential to reversing the deterioration due to current agricultural practices.

Upon completion of this study, it is apparent that there are certain basic planning concepts that could be applied in many parts of Nigeria to maintain a healthy development process that does not endanger natural resources. The strategies are as follows:

1. Any agricultural and development projects should accommodate the role of local citizens who are well informed on the importance of ecological balance.

2. Agricultural development or any kind of development should enhance the physical and biological equilibrium of the land.

3. There should always be an attempt by all participating in agricultural endeavor and development to optimize the productivity of the land but minimize destruction and waste.

4. The federal, state, and local governments should devise a system of land use (this could be done through land reforms) that will enhance developments to benefit the society at large.

10 THE FUTURE

ENVIRONMENTAL AWARENESS

The African savannas and forests have undergone immense changes over the last sixty years. The savanna's subjection to grazing causes the replacement of more productive perennial grass species by lower-producing, less palatable perennials and annuals, bushes, and weeds. As mentioned in an earlier chapter, the thorny bushes are not good for cattle and do not protect the soil from erosion. The effect of heavy grazing on the botanical composition of the African natural pasture can be seen in the countries along the southern edges of the Sahara. Several research publications and reports have described the decline in ecological diversity in these countries. Wherever grazing is intensive, weeds take over. Natural coastal pastures of West Africa are known to have lost their valuable grass species and are now covered by lower-producing bushes and weeds.

Overgrazing by livestock, slashing and burning by the farmers who practice shifting cultivation, and excess logging all leave the African soil subjected to the problem of erosion. Generally the savannas of Africa are low in nitrogen content. The burning and erosion destroy the nitrogen-fixing bacteria of the soil. Erosion is a serious problem to the African savanna, and since most of the people of the savanna region depend on agriculture for their livelihood, the erosion problem must be tackled effectively by farmers, private enterprises involved in agriculture, and local and national governments. Tree planting must be pursued in an aggressive manner because of the important role of forestry in the economic development of the savanna region, although a sound appraisal of African resources must first be done, as there is currently a lack of sufficient and reliable data on forest produce. Certain types and qualities of wood are in limited supply over much of the savanna region, and in order to meet the present and future requirements, reliable data concerning the exact amount of species of plants available and the rate of exploitation is needed.

Reforestation programs can ease the enormous problem of ecological decline, but in order to be effective, such reforestation or crop transfer efforts should take into account the issue of species selection. Experience in several countries, such as Nigeria and Senegal, has shown that the planting of trees is a complex endeavor precisely because of regional differences. In choosing species, the following criteria must be considered: (1) the adaptability of the species in the new African environment; (2) the suitability of the produce; (3) ease of handling (some crop species are difficult to handle in the nursery and demand technical experience); (4) cropping ability to achieve the required quality and quantity; and (5) the availability of seeds. Proper management of the resources of the savanna region will enable Africa to meet the demands of an increasing population (both human and livestock) and to offer a higher standard of living (by African standards) to its people.

PUBLIC AND PRIVATE GLOBAL ASSISTANCE

There are several alternatives for Africa in terms of managing its resources. Predictions based on the capability of Africa to provide its own food indicate that the continent could be self-sufficient, as it was several decades ago. The problem began with the African governments' misdirected priorities of and the unnatural division of Africa by the "colonial masters." There is a need to educate the indigenous people of Africa in resource management and to confront the problems of modernity. There is demand for skilled and unskilled labor. For example, in Nigeria, which is one of the few African countries with a number of outstanding scholars, there is a need for people with technical expertise. There is also a shortage of agricultural specialists in Africa.

Foreign aid has provided a temporary solution to the deteriorating situation in Africa. Food aid has given immediate relief to the food shortages, and loans from the world bank may provide money for the start of projects, but past experience indicates that there have been problems with recurrent costs of development projects in Africa, and a lack of adequate provision for the maintenance of projects.

Most experts seem to agree that there is an increasing dependence on food imports and a high level of malnutrition in Africa. International efforts must focus on assisting African nations in (1) fighting deforestation, (2) fighting drought, (3) fighting desertification, (4) developing strategies for economic development, (5) establishing politically stable governments, (6) providing farmers with incentives to remain in agriculture, (7) agriculture research, (8) water resources management, and (9) land-use planning.

In 1986, the Food and Agriculture Organization (FAO) concluded in its regional conference that the ecological decline in Africa must be arrested quickly. If the present trends are allowed to continue, chronic famine will become widespread throughout the continent. In attempting to reverse the current trends, the FAO recommends that the following steps be taken: (1) Policies must be instituted by the African governments to improve the environment; (2) farmers' support must be improved substantially; and (3) the external economic environment must be improved in order for developing nations to raise the standard of living of their peoples.

A permanent solution should be sought to the recurring drought problem. Several countries in Africa are receiving international aid in order to provide food to the citizens. Rainfall affects water regimes in swamps, riverine areas, and flood plains, places that constitute agricultural lands for the cultivation of rice. In the last decade, the rice yields of these ecosystems have been adversely affected during the drought. Agriculture failure will continue to persist in Africa as long as the cultivated lands depend only on rain. Several countries will have to adopt aggressive plans to establish irrigation projects in order to remedy the African agrarian crisis. For example, the Sierra Leone government has adopted plans for massive rice production on a commercial basis. This scheme, which is located in the Gbondapi area of the Pujehun district, could be a model for the rest of the country and maybe Africa as a whole. International efforts, with assistance from international agencies such as the Food and Agriculture Organization, seem to suggest that with coordinated assistance, Africa could recover from sluggishness or stagnation in its food production.

Rice is becoming increasingly important in the African diet. For instance, in both Senegal and Nigeria people have become more dependent on rice. Some say that in Nigeria only the wealthy can afford to purchase rice. Because the importation of large quantities of rice puts a burden on their already dismal economies, these two countries are now trying to encourage domestic rice production. Due to irrigation costs, Senegal and Nigeria may not be able to produce enough rice for their domestic consumption. African governments must educate the public about the importance of variety in their diet; influencing eating habits could be one of the solutions to solving the African food crisis.

In order to proceed, the following problem situations in Africa need to be corrected: (1) food production is growing at a slower pace than the increase in population; (2) the desert of the Sahel region is expanding because of the alarming rate at which the resources are being used without careful planning; (3) deforestation is spreading; (4) export crops are static or declining; (5) the level of foreign debts have attained alarming levels; and (6) the terms of trade are not favorable to African nations. Although international assistance has increased, many African nations are still not making enough progress toward economic recovery. Perhaps the right development projects are not being emphasized? It is worthwhile to examine some of the efforts being carried out by international organizations and some African nations to provide a brighter future for Africa.

Several organizations and governments have been involved in the effort to assist African countries in dealing with their ailing economies. In 1980, the World Bank attempted to deal directly with West Africa's problems. The deteriorating economic situations in many Third World countries has forced many lending institutions in the industrialized nations to reassess their cooperation with developing countries. Many countries, such as Nigeria, Ghana, Sierra Leone, Guinea, Senegal, Mali, and Kenya, now find themselves in great debt to the World Bank and some developed countries (United Nations 1986).

In 1974, the United Nations General Assembly adopted the Declaration for the Establishment of a New International Economic Order (NIEO). This economic cooperation basically outlined the basis upon which the industrialized nations will assist the developing countries. The issues centered upon (1) commodity agreements, (2) trade, (3) flows of concessionary assistance, (4) generalized debt relief, (5) reform of the international monetary system, (6) more rapid industrialization of the developing world, (7) transfers of technology, (8) provision of assured and affordable supplies of food grains, and (9) the establishment of a new Law of the Sea, which will deal with issues related to resource development, such as the exploitation of underwater mineral resources.

The World Bank's research has shown that developing countries can improve their agricultural production primarily through research. Investing in agricultural research can lead to improvement of many facets of crop production. Unfortunately, up until the beginning of 1980, many African nations were investing only a small percentage of their agricultural expenditure on research. World Bank's data indicate that the industrialized countries spent between 1 and 2 percent of their agricultural gross national product (GNP) on agricultural research in 1975, while the developing countries spent only 0.31 percent in the same year. There has to be a substantial increase in research in order for developing nations to attain self-sufficiency in food production. While crop yields in countries such as the United States, Japan, Mexico, and Brazil have increased by about fourfold, crop yields in African countries have declined on the average.

In an attempt to be self-sufficient, some African countries are investigating the possibility of having an integrated rural development scheme. Ghana has succeeded in establishing such a program, called the Upper Regional Agricultural Development Program (URADP). Another rural development effort was carried out in Rivers State of Nigeria. The program was called School to Land and was established in 1984 as an endeavor toward producing enough food for the people of Rivers State of Nigeria. The state encourages people to volunteer to participate in the program and has been able to cultivate over 2,500 acres of land through the scheme. The participants are trained in different aspects of farming. The state-run program is mainly for high-school graduates whose academic credentials offer little or no possibility of university acceptance and who are dedicated to farming as a profession.

In order to encourage the individuals participating in this program to remain in agriculture, the Rivers State government has taken the following steps: (1) eighty-five percent of the income from the sale of the produce is paid to the farmers in twelve monthly installments; (2) machinery is provided to the farmers initially without a fee, but eventually, after the farmers have established themselves, the tractors and other equipment are rented out to them; and (3) the government is working out a process whereby the farmers eventually become landowners, because past experience has shown that farmers put more effort into developing a piece of land that belongs to them than they would if the cultivated land was leased to them (*West Africa* 1985).

In order for Africa to be self-sufficient in the future, research must catch up with advancements in agriculture, technology, medicine, and all other facets of development. Research is not being conducted as aggressively as it should be in many African countries because of financial and technical constraints. Many of these countries do not allocate adequate funds to research and there is a steady decline in foreign research monies.

Nonetheless, a few organizations are still trying to do the best they can in order to find better ways of producing food. Such an organization is the Consultative Group on International Agricultural Research (CGIAR), which supports research centers that deal with African agriculture. These centers include the International Institute of Tropical Agriculture (IITA) based in Ibadan, Nigeria; the International Livestock Center for Africa (ILCA) in Ethiopia; the International Laboratory for Research on Animal Diseases (ILRAD) in Kenya; the West African Rice Development Association (WARDA) in Liberia; and the International Crops Research Institute for the Semi-Arid Tropics (ICRISAT). These centers have been conducting important and useful research despite the economic and technological constraints they face.

Another area where research is seriously needed is in weather prediction. Knowledge of the climatic trends in Africa must be given high priority in order to combat the drought problem. In order to understand the severity of the lack of meteorological data in Africa, one needs only to examine the problem in the Sahel countries. The data in these countries are sparse and unreliable. Because of the lack of technical expertise in some of these countries, there are numerous errors in the recording of the data. Lack of expertise in information storage and retrieval management, negligence on the part of those with responsibility for data management, and destruction due to civil unrest also make the problem of weather prediction cumbersome. For example, the meteorological data for Chad were obliterated in the civil war that country faced in the 1980s. Ethiopia and Sudan experienced a neglect of recording of meteorological data because of preoccupation with their civil wars.

Research has an important role to play in the future of agriculture in Africa. Research will definitely enhance the establishment of a good agricultural base, which is of utmost importance in self-sufficiency.

One of the successes of research was reported in 1986, a compost method of combating drought in the desert. This is a soil regeneration method that is basically a controlled fermentation of organic waste. The end product is a fertilizer of high grade that has a high water-retaining capability. This product is apparently better than chemical fertilizers, since it does not cause erosion and soil degradation. It has the property of being able to hold an amount of water equivalent to three times its weight. The success of the product has been shown in small- and large-scale agriculture in Burkina Faso. Since the product is being produced locally, it is cheaper than imported fertilizers, and thus can be used by a large number of farmers in Africa. Other African countries where agricultural and animal by-products are available can use these by-products as fertilizers. Such attempts could enhance projects similar to Operation Feed the Nation in Nigeria or other "green revolutions." But it must be cautioned that similar projects should have an aim, proper management, and be devoid of corruption (*West Africa* 1986).

Other research areas that are important in seeking food self-sufficiency are nutrition and chemical food treatment. The latter has a very significant role to play in the preservation of food. For example, irradiation could assist in solving the food crisis in many developing countries. In this process that subjects food products to low doses of radiation, a change occurs in the molecular structure of the food that preserves it.

The feeding of Africa's growing population is not as overwhelming as it may seem. A study of the crop production potential of Africa's soils by the FAO in 1981 shows that even though 47 percent of Africa's land surface is not productive, African soils have the potential to produce enough food for the population. It is important, however, to invest in a separate research of food as opposed to focusing on crops in order to develop new ways to serve and prepare traditional crops. This endeavor will encourage the urban populations to buy more African foods instead of depending on foreign, imported foods.

The greatest African famine period of the century probably occurred in 1985, because of the prolongation of the 1982–84 drought and of food destruction by pestilence. Several countries in Africa are now strengthening existing programs and establishing new ones to help them in their struggle for self-sufficiency. Before examining examples of such programs in a few of the African countries, the constraints on agriculture should first be categorized into three major groups: (1) negative policies and priorities in agriculture; (2) lack of innovation, efficiency, relevant projects, and honesty; and (3) food aid from international agencies, such as the World Food Program (WFP) and foreign governments which is sold locally to neighboring countries without ever reaching its destinations. Thus starvation and hunger linger for long periods of time, resulting in death and malnutrition.

Mali's food strategy is worth mentioning here precisely because it exemplifies an attempt by an African government to develop a plan of agricultural self-sufficiency. The Malian program is very comprehensive because it has proven to be beneficial to both rural food producers and urban dwellers. In the program, the government keeps grain prices as low as possible but high enough to allow the rural producers to make a profit, thus encouraging them to increase their productivity of food crops. In other African countries without similar plans, the citizens spend a substantial part of their income on food. Some cannot afford to live on their monthly wages because of high cost of food. In countries where government regulations do not allow the farmers to make any profit on the food crops, the peasant farmers have turned to growing export crops (e.g., tobacco) that give them the opportunity to make a profit. These countries must develop strategies of helping their farmers to develop their land, better ploughing methods, and distribution of seeds and fertilizers, and must offer stable and suitable prices for food crops through cooperative societies. Such efforts will generate national survival and stability in the future. This does not mean that cash crops should be neglected, but that greater emphasis must be placed on the production of food crops in order to build political and economic security for the future.

In the past, Ghana and Nigeria received substantial amounts of foreign income through the cocoa industry. In recent years, this industry has suffered tremendously due to neglect and the decline in price. Since the cocoa industry was important to some of the rural economies in Ghana and Nigeria, its decline has already begun in several countries, such as Niger and Mali. As was mentioned earlier, the food irradiation process, which involves exposing food such as cocoa to low doses of radiation, can reverse the decline of the cocoa industry. Food irradiation is ideal for cocoa preservation because it will prolong cocoa's decaying period, thus enabling cocoa to be processed before spoilage. This process of irradiation is being practiced in South Africa, and The International Atomic En-

ergy Agency is planning to establish irradiation in twenty-five countries—
many of which are developing countries.

The real problem facing African nations is how to integrate Western
technology into their traditional ways of resource management. It is certainly essential that modern technological knowledge and skills should be
acquired by the indigenous peoples of Africa, but certain cautious steps
must be followed in order to make technological transfers successful. The
transfer of agricultural technology from the industrialized countries
should only be used to supplement the existing traditional methods of African agriculture. But it should not be a replacement, because there is danger in adopting foreign farming techniques out of context. Traditional
African farming has withstood the test of time; replacing the traditional
methods of agriculture with foreign, mechanized agricultural practices
poses a great danger to the environment. Experiences in the Sierra Leone
upland with rice production and in Kenya agriculture substantiate the argument that when mechanized agriculture is not carefully and properly
introduced into the African ecosystem, the result can be disastrous. These
two countries showed drops in crop production in successive years, as well
as loss in soil fertility and erosion.

Although Africa is in its fourth decade of independence, many of the
countries have not been able to develop the means of managing their resources, let alone to achieve self-sufficiency. The policymakers usually
give priority to one overwhelming problem at a time while the magnitude
of smaller problems increases. There should be a means of solving these
problems systematically.

CONCLUSIONS AND RECOMMENDATIONS

In this chapter, an attempt has been made to focus attention on the future of resource management in Africa with particular emphasis on the
self-sufficiency of agriculture. It must be reiterated that self-sufficiency
can be achieved in Africa with proper management of the African resources and the education of the public. Other steps that must be taken
are (1) to develop the capacity to produce subsistence crops in large quantities; (2) to diversify crop production in order to stimulate the export capabilities; (3) to expand the forestry industry to encourage reforestation;
(4) to modernize and improve farming techniques through research on a
continuous basis; (5) to include environmental programs in elementary
and high-school curricula so that young people are aware of the importance of ecological balance; (6) to encourage regional and subregional
projects, such as those suggested in the "Lagos Plan for the Economic Development of Africa"; (7) to mobilize the labor-intensive culture of Africa
in the restoration of soil and water resources; (8) to establish food reserve
systems for the bulk storage and preservation of food.

If African nations are successful in implementing the above-mentioned steps, the continent will have a brighter future in its agricultural sector, there will be a rise in nutritional levels, and there will be nonstagnation in export crop production.

11 SUMMARY OF PROGRAMS AND TOOLS

When one thinks of development by industrialized or Western standards, African development emerges with an almost confused definition; one may even go as far as to say that Africa's development is like an unfinished project. As Pisani (1987:4) notes:

The vast majority of cities in Africa are like giant suburbs without any equipment, no real centre, no organization. Sometimes they exist without a municipal administration, without finances. Cancerous blossoms. So lively however, so full of ingenuity, movement, dreams, work and passions. An admirable people live there and improvise life, where we would only get lost.

In the early 1970s, Africa's development was linked to its raw materials, and subsequently African countries and foreign investors determined Africa's future based on natural resources. This was a big mistake because current condition in many African countries are the net result of mismanagement and the abuse of resources. The future of Africa must now harness its resources and use them wisely. It should be a comprehensive, systematic, and methodological approach to resource utilization. Pisani (1987:5) succinctly suggests that this future should incorporate the following elements:

1. priority of agriculture and rural life;
2. education and professional training;
3. revival and adapted protection of the interior markets;
4. savings and investments;

5. human rights, civil society, responsibility, and democracy; and

6. transparency of political choices, so that all get involved.

It will not suffice if all the above-mentioned steps are taken without understanding that African development, through proper resource management, can only be achieved if the countries become self-sufficient rather than import-oriented.

An important area of emphasis should concern the disappearance of forest. Wolf (1987) has demonstrated in his work in South America that forest can be grown from scratch. This example can be emulated and duplicated in many parts of the developing world where deforestation and desertification are problems.

And whatever programs or tools are devised to address the issue of resource development and management in Africa, the role of women must have an integral part in order for progress to be achieved. Women are involved at the grass roots in the agricultural production of many Third World countries. The success of any program aimed at solving the problem of food inadequacy in Africa must involve women. Women should play more prominent roles in the development of strategies to manage resources, including the implementation phase of programs.

Although in many parts of the developing world, especially in Africa, the number of children one has is perceived in terms of wealth and status, a large number of children in families decreases the overall quality of life for the family and for the nation as a whole. Educating both men and women about family planning issues is of great importance.

There are many arguments for and against aid in the process of development of Africa. Aid is important to Africa's development—if there are little or no strings attached. If the aid is in the best interest of Africa, the needs of the people will be served. It should also be pointed out that the aid provided by the developed countries is not enough by any standard. In order for effective development to take place, it must be sustained.

A gradual exchange of goods, along with knowledge, will help ensure a positive transition to achieve self-sufficiency. Aid is most beneficial when human needs are fulfilled. Not only must hunger and thirst be quenched, but the ability to eliminate the cause of the problem must also be achieved. A gradual withdrawal of provided goods should be replaced with the ability to produce goods independently in the future. It is important to stress that some of Africa's difficulties with its development programs are due in part to the repayment arrangement with the International Monetary Fund (IMF).

The United Nations has been attempting to find permanent solutions to Africa's problems. Berg (1987:16) eloquently claims that, among other things, the following should be done:

1. We must tap the world's surplus for Africa;

2. the United States must accompany the qualitative reorientation of its aid program to Africa with much greater financial backing;

3. the Soviet Union must play a more prominent role in Africa's development; and

4. African countries and foreign donors must strive to increase the quality of their development projects.

It should be pointed out that aid should not in any way undermine the self-reliance goals of African countries. Past experience with foreign aid suggests that development aid discourages the innovative and creative motivation of African governments because external factors affect Africa's capability to develop its resources. With special assistance from international organizations and donor countries, and with a new North-South trade and monetary order, Africa will be able to have programs that will address the high birth rate, speed up economic growth, increase agricultural production, and enhance industrial production.

The continuing efforts of the FAO are significant. Africa has benefited from a wide range of programs, such as planning, management, development, improvement of farming systems, improvement of agricultural products, establishment of agro-based factories, and the research projects that benefit animal production and health (WHO 1984). These efforts should continue on a permanent basis to ensure the stability and continuity of agriculture production.

In Chapter 4 the water problem was discussed at length. It must be emphasized that one of the obstacles to economic development is the lack of water (both in quantity and quality). The International Drinking Water Supply and Sanitation Decade aimed at providing safe drinking water to everyone on earth by 1990. Based on the current global water situation, it did not achieve this goal. However, progress could be made toward achieving the goal at a later date if the following steps, as suggested by the World Health Organization (1984), are taken:

1. development of underground water through improved boreholes,

2. construction of small earth dams,

3. surface water conservation schemes,

4. repair and maintenance facilities for existing water development projects and plants,

5. cartographic and remote sensing work to identify new water resources,

6. early warning systems for drought and the development of water reservoirs for emergency situations, and

7. afforestation and reafforestation of river banks and water-heads to improve river water flows.

The African infrastructure, like those of many other developing regions of the world, deserves a lot of maintenance, redevelopment, and planning. Although many African countries have added new roads to the ones constructed by the colonial rulers, the roads are poorly maintained. These roads do not encourage intra-African trade; hence resources in rural communities are not properly utilized and protected. Several meetings by African government officials have produced an agreement to establish projects for the maintenance and rehabilitation of existing roads. There will also be projects that will enhance economic relations and development of African nations. This endeavor is estimated to cost about $9.2 billion over a ten-year period (Wa Muthanik 1987).

It is possible for African nations to develop their resources efficiently and adequately. With the new commitment of the international community, Africa's resources could be preserved indefinitely. The United Nation's General Assembly is committed to this course, as demonstrated by the following actions: (1) It has established Africa's Priority Program for Economic Recovery 1986–1990, and (2) it focuses development efforts on agriculture and food production.

The efforts of the Institute for Natural Resources in Africa (INRA) in making sure that African resources are preserved and conserved are worth noting. There are four basic areas where the INRA is involved:

1. Biotechnology techniques to improve the yield of some crops that will solve some of the food problems of the continent.
2. Projects of germ plasma distribution to alleviate the problem of deforestation, desertification, and the loss of endemic species.
3. Land-use systems that can promote the economic development of Africa without jeopardizing its resources. Local involvement is significant in this effort.
4. Systemic and ecologically sensitive techniques of harnessing Africa's raw materials without destroying the ecosystem.

With the assistance of international organizations, donor countries, and the admirable spirit of the African people, the ecological decline can be reversed and Africa can find a path to economic recovery.

APPENDIX: QUESTIONNAIRE USED IN SURVEY ON RESOURCE MANAGEMENT PROBLEMS IN NIGERIA

Please Circle the Appropriate Response.

1. Which of the following best describes your opinion about the agricultural practice in Nigeria?

    a. Poor

    b. Fair

    c. Good

    d. Excellent

    e. No response

2. Do you think Nigeria should embark on mechanized agriculture in order to feed the growing population?

    a. Yes

    b. No

    If no, which of the following should occur?

    a. Intensify their current agricultural practice.

    b. Have a combination of mechanized and traditional agricultural systems.

    c. Other (please specify).

3. Agricultural practices in Nigeria have led to the destruction of the forests and savannas.

    a. Strongly agree

    b. Agree

    c. Don't know

    d. Disagree

    e. Strongly disagree

4. The political instability in Nigeria exacerbates agricultural problems.

   a. Strongly agree

   b. Agree

   c. Don't know

   d. Disagree

   e. Strongly disagree

5. There is not enough research conducted to improve the quality and quantity of food production in Nigeria.

   a. Strongly agree

   b. Agree

   c. Don't know

   d. Disagree

   e. Strongly disagree

6. Present practices such as logging for timber and firewood are increasing the problem of deforestation.

   a. Strongly agree

   b. Agree

   c. Don't know

   d. Disagree

   e. Strongly disagree

7. Agricultural problems could be ameliorated in many parts of Nigeria if population increase were checked.

   a. Strongly agree

   b. Agree

   c. Don't know

   d. Disagree

   e. Strongly disagree

8. The lack of management skills is one of the problems facing Nigeria with regard to resource management.

   a. Strongly agree

   b. Agree

   c. Don't know

   d. Disagree

   e. Strongly disagree

9. Nigeria is providing the necessary environment conducive for international involvement in the management of their resources.

   a. Strongly agree

   b. Agree

c. Don't know

d. Disagree

e. Strongly disagree

10. The demand for the natural resources of Nigeria in the industrialized countries encourages the exploitation of natural resources.

a. Strongly agree

b. Agree

c. Don't know

d. Disagree

e. Strongly disagree

11. The Nigerian government takes the issues of conservation and preservation seriously.

a. Strongly agree

b. Agree

c. Don't know

d. Disagree

e. Strongly disagree

12. How would you rate the urgency of combating natural resource destruction in "developing countries" like Nigeria?

a. Very urgent

b. Urgent

c. Not urgent

d. No opinion

13. The problem of soil degradation due to deforestation has reached alarming proportions in many parts of the country.

a. Strongly agree

b. Agree

c. Don't know

d. Disagree

e. Strongly disagree

14. Regional and international cooperations are necessary in order to tackle the problem of resource abuse in a developing country like Nigeria.

a. Strongly agree

b. Agree

c. Don't know

d. Disagree

e. Strongly disagree

15. Which of the following do you think is/are the major problem(s) facing agriculture in a developing country such as Nigeria?

   a. Lack of technical expertise on modern agricultural methods.

   b. Few people in the agro-business.

   c. Lack of incentives to enter agriculture business.

   d. The poor condition of the soil.

   e. A combination of a, b, c, and d.

16. Nomadic pastoralism should be abandoned in order to prevent vegetation destruction.

   a. Strongly agree

   b. Agree

   c. Don't know

   d. Disagree

   e. Strongly disagree

17. Alternative energy sources for domestic use should be aggressively pursued by developing nations (instead of firewood).

   a. Strongly agree

   b. Agree

   c. Don't know

   d. Disagree

   e. Strongly disagree

18. Nigeria should cease depending on imported food.

   a. Strongly agree

   b. Agree

   c. Don't know

   d. Disagree

   e. Strongly disagree

19. Nigeria must embark on large-scale food production instead of depending upon subsistence agriculture.

   a. Strongly agree

   b. Agree

   c. Don't know

   d. Disagree

   e. Strongly disagree

20. Education of rural farmers on issues of ecological balance should be a top priority of the developing nations' effort to discourage biological equilibrium disturbance.

   a. Strongly agree

   b. Agree

   c. Don't know

   d. Disagree

   e. Strongly disagree

REFERENCES

Abdin, G. 1948. "Physical and Chemical Investigations Relating to Algal Growth in the River Nile." *Cairo Bulletin Institute of Egypt* 29:19–44.

Adeyoju, Kolade S. 1975. *Forestry and the Nigerian Economy.* Ibadan, Nigeria: Ibadan University Press.

Allen, J. C., and Barnes, D. F. 1985. "The Causes of Deforestation in Developing Countries." *Annals of the Association of American Geographers* 75:163–84.

Ashcraft, Norman. 1973. *Colonialism and Underdevelopment.* New York: Teachers College Press, Columbia University.

Ayadike, Obinna. 1988. "Toxic Terrorism." *West Africa* (June 20):1108–11, 1144.

Bale, John, and Drakakis-Smith, David. 1988. *Tourism and Development in the Third World.* London: Routledge.

Baumann, H. 1928. "The Division of Work According to Sex in African Hoe Culture." *Africa* 1 (1):289–319.

Beadle, L. C. 1974. *The Inland Waters of Tropical Africa: An Introduction to Tropical Limnology.* New York: Longman.

Beale, J. G. 1975. *The Manager and the Environment: General Theory and Practice of Environmental Management.* New York: Pergamon Press.

Berg, Robert J. 1987. "Not the Devil, but Not the Angel: Foreign Aid in Africa." *Journal of the Society for International Development* 2 (3):128–140.

Biersteker, Thomas J. 1978. *Distortion or Development? Contending Perspectives on the Multinational Corporation.* Cambridge: MIT Press.

Binzangi, K. 1985. "Wood as a Source of Fuel in Upper Shaba (Zaire)." *The Commonwealth Forestry Review* 64 (3):227–37.

Bongarts, John. 1987. "End of Population Explosion in the Third World." *California Aggie,* February 20. 6–7.

Boserup, E. 1970. *Women's Role in Economic Development.* New York: St. Martin's Press.

Britton, Stephen G. 1981. "Tourism Dependency and Development: A Mode Analysis." *Occasional Paper*, No. 23. Canberra: Development Studies Center, Australian National University.

Brown, J. B. 1978. *Lusaka Fuelwood Project.* Ndola, Zambia: Forestry Department. Stenciling document.

Browning, G. M., and Parish, C. L. 1947. "A Method for Determining the Use and Limitations of Rotation and Conservation Practices in the Control of Soil Erosion in Iowa." Journal of American Society of Agronomy 39: 65–73.

Buringh, P. 1979. *Introduction to the Study of Soils in Tropical and Subtropical Regions.* Wageningen, The Netherlands: Center for Agricultural and Publishing Documentation.

Cahen, L. 1954. *Géologie du Congo Belge* (Geology of the Belgian Congo). Liège, Belgium: Vaillant Carmanne.

Cobern, William W. 1983. "Nomadism and Education: The Erosion in Iowa." *Journal of American Society of Agronomy* 39:65–73. Fulani Dilemma." *West Africa,* April 4. 832–34.

Coursey, D. G. 1976. "Origins and Domestication of Yams in Africa." In *Origins of African Plant Domestication,* ed. J. R. Harlan, J. M. J. deWet, and A. B. L. Stemler, pp. 383–408. The Hague–Paris: Mouton.

Curry-Lindahl, Kai. 1972. *Conservation for Survival.* New York: William Morrow.

Dadson, J. A. 1983. "Ghana: Food and the Nation." *West Africa,* July 18. 1596–97, 1659–83.

DeSanto, R. S. 1978. *Concepts of Applied Ecology.* New York: Springer-Verlag.

Doyle, Mark. 1983. "Bush Fires Devastate Farmlands." *West Africa,* April 4. 821.

Driberg, J. H. 1932. "The Status of Women among Nilotics and Hilo-Hamitics." *Africa*: 3:404–21.

Duncan, O. D. 1969. "Human Ecology and Population Studies." In *The Study of Population,* ed. P. M. Hauser and O. D. Duncan. Chicago: University of Chicago Press.

Eicher, Carl K. 1986. *Transforming African Agriculture.* Report No. 4. New York: The Hunger Project.

Feldman, Marcus. 1987. "End of Population Explosions in the Third World." *California Aggie,* February 20. 6–8.

Floyd, B. 1969. *Eastern Nigeria.* London: Macmillan.

Food and Agriculture Organization/Unesco 1973. *Maps of Major Soils of the World.* Paris: FAO.

———. 1978. *Methodology for Assessing Soil Degradation.* Rome: FAO.

———. 1980. *FAO Production Yearbook.* Vol. 34. Rome: FAO.

———. 1981a. *Crop Production Potential of African Soils.* Paris: FAO.

———. 1981b. *Tropical Forest Resources Assessment Project (in the Framework of Gems: Forest Resources of Africa, Part 2).* Technical Report 2, Un 32/6, 1301-78-04. Rome: FAO and UNEP.

———. 1982. FAO Production Yearbook. Vol. 36. 62. Rome: FAO.

———. 1983. *FAO Production Yearbook.* Vol. 37. Rome: FAO.

Forsberg, F. R. 1977. "Man's Effect on Island Ecosystem." In *Global Perspectives on Ecology,* ed. Thomas Emmel. Palo Alto: Mayfield. 20–37.

Foy, Colm. 1980. "Regrowth of Angola." *West Africa,* August 11. 1475–76.

Frankel, O. H., and Soule, M. E. 1981. *Conservation and Evolution.* Cambridge, United Kingdom: Cambridge University Press.

Gander, M. V. 1984. "Wood as a Source of Fuel in South Africa." *South African Forestry Journal* 6:1–9.

Golley, Frank B. 1975. *Tropical Ecological Systems.* New York: Springer-Verlag.

Grove, A. T. 1985. *The Niger and Its Neighbors.* Rotterdam, The Netherlands: Belkema.

Hammerton, D. 1972. "The Nile River: A Case History." In *River Ecology and Man,* ed. Ray T. Oglesby, Clarence A. Carlson, and James A. McCann. New York: Academic Press.

Harlan, Jack R., DeWet, Jan M., and Stember, Ann B. 1976. *Origins of African Plant Domestication.* The Hague–Paris: Mouton.

Harris, D. R. 1976. "Traditional Systems of Plant Production and Origins of Agriculture in West Africa." In *Origins of African Plant Domestication,* ed. J. R. Harlan, J. M. J. deWet, and A. B. L. Stemler, pp. 311–56. The Hague–Paris: Mouton.

Haviden, M. A. 1975. "The History of Cultivation in West Africa: A Bibliographical Guide." *World Economics and Rural Sociology Abstracts* 17: 423–37.

Heller, Robert. 1962. *Geology and Earth Sciences.* New York: Holt, Rinehart & Winston.

Henderson-Sellers, H. 1981. "The Effect of Land Clearance and Agricultural Practices upon Climate." In *Blowing in the Wind: Deforestation and Long-Range Implications,* ed. Vinson H. Sutlive, Nathan Altshuler, and Mario D. Zamora. Williamsburg, Virginia: College of William and Mary.

Hickling, C. F. 1961. *Tropical Inland Fisheries.* London: Longman.

Hopkins, B. 1973. *Vegetation of the Olukemeji Forest Reserve in Nigeria.* Ibadan, Nigeria: University Press.

Husbands, Winston. 1989. "Social Status and Perception of Tourism in Zambia." *Annals of Tourism Research* 16(689):37–53.

Imerbore, A. M. A. 1967. "Hydrology of Eleryele Reservoir, Nigeria." *Hydrobiologia* 33:161–85.

International Union for the Conversation of Nature and Natural Resources (IUCN). 1980. *World Conservation Strategy.* Gland, Switzerland. IUCN.

James, Valentine U. 1987a. "The Need for Adequate Resource Management in Africa." Paper presented at the New York African Studies Association's Annual Conference, Africa and America Bridging the Gaps, Mercy College, Dobbs Ferry, N.Y.

———.1987b. "Traditional Systems of Resource Management and Threats to Biological Systems in Developing Countries." Paper presented at the Conference on Famine Complex and Women: Culture, History, and Science. Bennett College, Greensboro, North Carolina.

Kimble, G. H. T. 1960. *Tropical Africa: Land and Livelihood.* Vol. 1. New York: Twentieth Century Fund.

Knuti, L. L., Korpi, M., and Hide, J. C. 1970. *Profitable Soil Management.* New York: Prentice-Hall.

Kulshrestha, S. K., and Mohammed, R. A. 1984. "Spatial Models for Regrouping of Villages in Nigeria." *Habitat International* 8:3–4.

Lall, S., and Streeten, P. 1977. *Foreign Investment, Transnationals and Developing Countries.* London: Macmillan.

Lambooy, J. G. 1969. *De Agrarische Hervorming in Tunesie: Proeve van een Social-geografisch Onderzoek* (Agrarian Reform in Tunisia). Assen: Van Gorcum.

Lesaca, Reynaldo R. 1974. "Pollution Control Legislation and Experience in a Developing Country: The Philippines." *Journal of Developing Countries* 8 (4). 147–63.

McNamara, Robert S. 1969. "Address to the Board of Governors of World Bank." Washington, D.C. World Bank.

Madeley, John. 1980. "UNDP Turns to the Rivers." *West Africa*, August 11. 1483–84.

Mathieson, A., and Wall, G. 1982. *Tourism: Economic, Physical, and Social Impacts.* Longman: NY.

Mattelart, Armand. 1983. *Transnationals and Third World Countries: The Struggle for Culture.* South Hadley, Mass. Bergin & Garvey.

Moldenhauer, W. C., and Amemiya, M. 1969. "Tillage Practices for Controlling Cropland Erosion." *Journal of Soil and Water Conservation* 24:19–21.

Monakov, A. V. 1968. "The Zooplankton and Zoobenthos of the White Nile and Adjoining Waters in the Sudan." *Hydrobiologia* 33:161–85.

Moorman, F. R., and Greenland, D. J. 1980. "Major Production Systems Related to Soil Properties in Humid Tropical Africa." *Priorities for Alleviating Soil Related Constraints to Food Production in the Tropics.* Manila: International Rice Research Institute, with Cornell University.

Moran, Theodore H. 1985. "Multinational Corporation and the Developing Countries: An Analytical Overview." In *Multinational Corporations,* ed. Theodore Moran. Lexington, Mass.: Lexington Books. 3–21.

Morgan, W. B., and Pugh, J. C. 1969. *Africa.* London: Methun.

Myers, Norman. 1984. *The Primary Source: Tropical Forests and Our Future.* New York: Norton.

Ngin Kwi, Soong, Haridas, G., Seng, Choou Yeoh, and Hua, Pen. 1980. *Soil Erosion and Conservation in Peninsula Malaysia.* Kuala Lumpur: Rubber Research Institute of Malaysia.

Obok, J. U. 1980. "Transportation Development and Urbanization: The Case of Calabar Municipality, Nigeria." *African Urban Studies* 7 (33). 171–89.

Okigbo, B. M. 1980. "Farming Systems of West Africa in Relation to Nitrogen Cycling." In *Nitrogen Cycling in West African Ecosystems,* ed. T. Rosswall. Sweden: Reklam and Katalogtryck.

Olembo, R. J. 1981. "Address from the Division of Environmental Management." In *The Ecology and Utilization of African Inland Waters,* ed. J. J. Symoens, M. Burgis, and J. J. Ganet. Nambi, Kenya: United Nations.

Olowo, Bola. 1989. "The Arms Debate," *West Africa,* May 1–7. 973.

Oyedipe, F. P. A. 1973. "Problems of Socio-economic Adjustment of Resettlers." *Kainji Lake Studies 2,* ed. A. L. Mabogunje. Ibadan: Niger.

Pala, Achola O. 1976. *African Women in Rural Development: Research Trends and*

Priorities. New York: Overseas Liaison Committee—American Council on Education.

Panrose, Edith T. 1959. "Profit Sharing between Producing Countries and Oil Companies in the Middle East." *Economic Journal,* 69 279:238–54.

Peil, Margaret, and Sada, Pius O. 1984. *African Urban Society.* New York: Wiley.

Pisani, Edgard. 1987. "Africa." *Journal of the Society for International Development* 2 (3). 45–56.

Presvelou, C. 1980. "Rural Women and Development Aid." In *The Household, Women and Agricultural Development,* ed. Clio Presvelou and Saskia Spijkers-Zwart. Proceedings of a symposium of Women in Agricultural Development. The University of Wageningen, The Netherlands: Department of Home Economics, Agricultural University of Wageningen.

Qadeer, Mohammad A. 1983. *Urban Development in the Third World: International Dynamics of Lahore, Pakistan.* New York: Praeger.

Raay, H. G. T. van. 1975. *Rural Planning in a Savanna Region.* Rotterdam, The Netherlands: Rotterdam University Press.

Revelle, R. 1976. "Energy Use in Rural India." *Science* 192:969–75.

Robert, M. 1946. *Le Congo Physique.* 3rd ed. Liège, Belgium: Vaillant Carmanne.

Rodney, Walter. 1974. *How Europe Underdeveloped Africa.* Washington, D.C.: Howard University Press.

Rupeley, Lawrence. 1980. "Farming Fiscally." *West Africa,* July 14. 1290–91.

Sadder, T. 1980. "River Basin Development and Local Initiative in African Savanna Environments." In *Human Ecology in Savanna Environments,* ed. D. R. Harris. London: Academic Press.

Science News. 1988. "African Elephants—A Dying Way of Life." May 21.

Scudder, T. 1966. "Man-made Lakes and Population Resettlement in Africa." In *Man-made Lakes,* ed. Lowe-McConnell, R. H. Symposium of the Institute of Biology. London: Cambridge Univ. 15:99–108.

Seaborg, Glen T. 1969. "The Environment and What to Do about It." Paper presented to a meeting of the National Academy of Sciences. Argonne National Laboratory. Argone, Ill.

Shaw, T. 1968. "Comment on 'Origins of African Agriculture,' by O. Davies, H. Hugot, and D. Seddon." *Current Anthropology* 8:500–501.

———. 1972. "Early Agriculture in Africa." *Journal of Historical Society of Nigeria* 6:143–91.

———. 1976. "Early crops in Africa: A Review of Evidence." In *Origins of African Plant Domestication,* ed. J. R. Harlan, J. M. J. deWet, and A. B. L. Stemler, pp. 197–253. The Hague–Paris: Mouton.

Sorokin, Pitirim, and Zimmerman, Carle C. 1929. *Principles of Rural-Urban Sociology.* New York: Holt.

Soule, M. E. and Wilcox, B. A. ed. 1980. *Conservation Biology: An Evolutionary-Ecological Perspective.* Sunderland, Mass.: Sinauer Associates.

Spedding, C. R. W. 1975. *The Biology of Agricultural Systems.* London: Academic Press.

Sports Illustrated. 1987. "The Rhino Wars." March 2. 12.

Swedner, Harold. 1960. *Ecological Differentiation of Habits and Attitudes.* New York: CWK Gleerup/Lund.

Talling, J. F., and Rzoska, H., Jr. 1967. "The Development of Plankton in Relation to Hydrologic Regime in the Blue Nile." *Journal of Ecology.* 55: 637–62.

Todaro, Michael. 1977. *Economic Development in the Third World.* New York: Longman.

———. 1985. *Economic Development in the Third World.* New York: Longman.

Troeh, Frederick, and Thompson, Louis M. 1978. *Soils and Soil Fertility.* New York: McGraw-Hill.

United Nations. 1986. *Survey of Economic and Social Conditions in Africa.* Geneva: United Nations.

U.S. Agency for International Development. 1985. "U.S. Strategy on the Conservation of Biological Diversity." An Interagency Task Force Report to Congress. Washington, D.C.: Office of Technology Assessment.

U.S. Office of Technology Assessment. 1983. "Sustaining Tropical Forest Resources." U.S. and International Institutions Background Paper No.2. Washington, D.C.: Office of Technology Assessment.

U.S. Conservation Service. 1972. *Soil Map of the World.* Washington, D.C.: The Soil Geography Unit of USSCS, 43.

Vernon, Raymond. 1986. "International Investment and International Trade in the Product Cycle." *Quarterly Journal of Economics* 80 (May). 306–14

Vernon, Raymond, and Wells, Louis T., Jr. 1986. *The Economic Environment of International Business.* Englewood Cliffs, N.J.: Prentice-Hall.

Visser, S. A., ed. 1970. *Kainji, A Nigerian Man-made Lake.* Niger Institute. Ibadan, Nigeria: University of Ibadan.

Walter, H. 1973. *Vegetation of the Earth in Relation to Climate and the Ecophysiological Conditions.* New York: Springer-Verlag.

Wa Muthanik, Bingu. 1987. "Special Assistance Needs for Africa, with Special Reference to Sub-Saharan Africa." *Journal of the Society for International Development.* 2 (3). 34.

Water Resources Council. 1973. "Establishment of Principles and Standards of Planning—Water and Related Land Resources." *Federal Registration* 38 (147) 33–49.

Wenner, Carl G. 1980. *Soil Conservation in Kenya: Especially in Small Scale Farming in High Potential Areas Using Labor Intensive Methods.* Nairobi: Ministry of Agriculture.

West Africa. 1980. "Mali's Economic Gloom." August 25. 1592–93.

———. 1981. "Nigeria's Critical Shortage of Skills." March 16. 543–44.

———. 1985. "Nigerian Agriculture: This Is Development." November 25. 2465–67.

———. 1986. "Financial Standing." February 11.

———. 1989. "The Conservation Alternative." December 4–10.

Wolf, Edward. 1987. "Growing Forest from Scratch." *Futurist* 7:41–42.

The World Bank. 1972. Tourism: Sector Working Paper. Washington, D.C.: World Bank.

———. 1981. *Statistical Yearbook.* New York: United Nations.

———. 1985a. *Trade and Development Report.* Paris: United Nations.

———. 1985b. *World Development Report.* New York: Oxford University Press.

———. 1985c. *Yearbook of Forest Products.* Rome: FAO.

World Health Organization. 1984. *The International Drinking Water Supply and Sanitation Decede.* Geneva: World Health Organization.

Worthington, E. B. 1958. "On the Evolution of Fish in the Lakes of Africa." *International Review of Hydrobiologia* 35:304–17.

———. 1970. "International Economic Relations and the Large International Firm." In *New Orientations: Essays in International Relations,* ed. E. F. Panrose, Peter Lyon, and Edith T. Panrose. New York: Humanities Press.

INDEX

ABOUT THE AUTHOR

VALENTINE U. JAMES, an Assistant Professor of Urban and Environmental Planning at the University of Virginia School of Architecture, specializes in Environmental Planning and has been teaching and writing about Third World development for several years. His research focuses on Sub-Saharan Africa. Dr. James is the editor of *Urban and Rural Development in Third World Countries.*